ON SACRED GROUND

Jewish and Christian Clergy
Reflect on Transformative Passages
from the Five Books of Moses

Edited by
JEFF BERNHARDT

BLACKBIRD BOOKS
NEW YORK • LOS ANGELES

A Blackbird Original, July 2012

Cover painting by Lois Fein
courtesy of The Vreeland Collection

Manufactured in the United States of America.

Cataloging-in-Publication Data

On sacred ground : Jewish and Christian clergy reflect on transformative
passages from the five books of Moses / edited by Jeff Bernhardt.
p. cm.
1. Bible. O.T. Five Books of Moses—Commentaries—Interfaith.
2. Bible. O.T. Five Books of Moses—Study and teaching—Interfaith.
3. Bible O.T. Five Books of Moses—Interpretation. I. Title.
BS1225.53 .B47 2012 222′.I07′082—dc22 2012944147

Blackbird Books
www.bbirdbooks.com
email us at editor@bbirdbooks.com

ISBN 978-1-61053-018-7

First Edition

10 9 8 7 6 5 4 3 2 1

To those who came before me,
who guided me and brought me closer to Torah:

Bess and Lou Schnell
Mitzie and Jerry Bernhardt

To those who take the journey with me—who teach me,
learn with me, and, I hope, learn from me:

Ruth and Henry Bernhardt
Alyssa and Bill Villari
Zachary, Benjamin, Jacob, and Rebecca Villari

To those who come after me:

I hope I have made a difference.

Contents

Introduction

And Jacob awoke from his sleep and said, "Surely the Eternal One is in this place and I did not know it."

Genesis 28:16

This is the verse from the Five Books of Moses that speaks to me and fills me with great awe and appreciation. Jacob dreams there is a ladder reaching from the earth to the heavens, with angels going up and down. Like a reassuring parent, God tells him in his dream, "I am with you." When Jacob awakes, he realizes that he is in fact resting on sacred ground.

This text reminds me that every place and every moment in time can be holy if only we live up to our own potential to make it so—in our words and in our actions, with the way we greet one another, and with the way we carry on in our relationships. We have the power and potential to bring holiness to any place, to any moment, to any intersection of space and time. God truly can be in *this* place. I not only know this, but I have the power to make it so. The challenge, of course, is to remember this and to make it an actuality as we each go forth into life every day.

In her book *Death Comes for the Archbishop*, Willa Cather writes, "The Miracles of the Church seem to me to rest not so much upon faces or voices or healing power coming suddenly near to us from afar off, but upon our perceptions being made finer, so that for a moment our eyes can see and our ears can hear what is there about us always." When I first read this, it echoed my understanding of Jacob's revelation after he awakens from his dream.

In this book, you will read the words of Jewish and Christian clergy, people who have chosen to make God's word an intimate part of their lives and their vocations. These men and women teach scripture and preach on the values that we learn from the text. The clergy who have contributed to this book represent a diversity of religious denominations, gender, background, age, and geography within North America. Some are just beginning their work as religious leaders while others are retired, some have been doing this work for many years, and some were in another field when they heard and responded to their calling. As well, they do their work in a variety of areas—chaplaincies, church and synagogue pulpits, agencies, organizations, and educational institutions.

Each clergyperson was asked to choose a verse or text from the Five Books of Moses. This particular section of the Bible was chosen as it is part of the canon for both Christians and Jews. Each contributor was invited to choose the passage which speaks to him or her in a personal way and then to explain why. Some interpreted this as the verse or text which he or she considers most important while in other cases it was understood to be a question of which text informs his or her life. The only limitations placed upon them was with regard to maximum length. It was also important to me that no language or contribution be offensive to any individual or group.

The translations of the chosen texts are based on the 1917 Jewish Publication Society English translation. I have attempted to adapt the language to a more modern translation (e.g. "thy" became "your") and also attempted to use a more gender neutral language when possible and at the same time to maintain as literal a translation as possible. One example is the use of "the Eternal One" in place of "the Lord." When the contributor uses a translation in the body of his or her response, the translation may differ, often because the particular translation he or she uses relates to why the verse was chosen in the first place. Likewise, there may be a difference in choice around some terminology, reference to God and to how God's name is written. Once determined that this was intentional and preferred by the contributor, this choice was respected. Therefore the contributions themselves may not be consistent with one another in some respects, and that simply is a further reflection of the diversity amongst the contributors. Where a contributor has chosen a longer text upon which to reflect (for example an entire chapter or narrative), I indicated this by using ellipses (. . .) to include the beginning and the end of the text selected.

The bios which follow each contributor's response were provided by each author.

My hope is that in addition to helping to create and fortify bridges across faiths and religious denominations, that this book will also strengthen our connection to scripture. As you read the reflections of the contributors, I encourage you to ask yourself, which verse or text from the Five Books of Moses speaks to you, inspires you, has come to impact the way you see or interact with the world or has the potential to do so.

May the reading of these reflections and the conversations they spark serve to connect us to one another and to those past, present, and future who recognize the fertile and sacred words of The Five Books of Moses, and may we each make them our own.

Jeff Bernhardt
Los Angeles
July 2012

GENESIS

In the beginning God created the heaven and the earth.

Genesis 1:1

Seeking a Return to the Garden

"In the Beginning." Genesis begins that way as does the Gospel of John which begins, "In the beginning with the word" (referring to the coming of Jesus Christ). Whether we are speaking with a Jewish voice or a Christian voice, we all have to speak from the beginning where we all have some commonality.

In Genesis, God created a special and unique human being, the crown of all His creation. In this first covenant God gave man the unique gift of being in His image—the gift of intellect, the gift of free will, and the gift of emotion. Man is made to create the way God, the Eternal Artist, continues to create. Man, however, used free will and disobeyed the covenant, and Adam and Eve were therefore driven from God's presence, from the ideal of the garden, of paradise. Man has always wanted to return to paradise, the place of delight.

The Book of Exodus represents the rebirth, the return to the garden (in this case the Holy Land) and to the presence of God, a new beginning. God's spirit is in every human being, and we long to reconnect to our creator. Through worship, through ritual, through our ritual clothing, we are expressing our desire to reconnect with God. Our behavior and our relationship to one another brings us closer to God.

I was a priest for twelve years and was going to throw it all away for fear that I was a phony. Before calling the bishop to tell him my plan, I went to Mt. Athos monastery in Greece. I went before an icon, and I began to pray, saying, "God, am I a phony? Lord, am I doing this just to make a living? Give me a sign."

All of a sudden I felt like I was in a trance—like I was paralyzed, I couldn't move my body, and I began to weep uncontrollably. It was a complete running of tears. As I stood in front of the icon, I felt a spiritual power compel me to take off the cross I was wearing, a cross given to me by my father etched with his name and his last words on the back of it. I was moved to place the cross on the icon. I then sat and spent what must have been six hours weeping. I was so overwhelmed with inner peace and joy. That night I slept so deeply and sweetly for the first time in so long that I felt a release and a Presence saying, "You are not wasting your time." I remembered Jesus' words to Peter in the scripture: "You have not chosen me, I have chosen you."

From then on everything seemed to open up. I don't think I'd be in my parish, in this place had it not been for that. I might have turned to other substances to anesthetize the emptiness within. I've had spiritual revelations like that from time to time at the most difficult moments. It is this revelation that keeps me going during challenging times. It was my reconnection to the garden.

Father John Bakas was born on the Greek island of Tinos. He was ordained as a Greek Orthodox priest in 1977. He has been dean of St. Sophia Cathedral in Los Angeles since 1995. He is a part-time faculty member at Loyola Marymount University Department of Theology.

And God said: "Let us make humankind in our image, after our likeness; and let them have dominion over the fish of the sea, and over the birds of the air, and over the wild animals, and over all the earth, and over every creeping thing that creeps upon the earth." And God created humankind in the divine image, in the image of God did God create him; male and female God created them. And God blessed them, and God said to them: "Be fruitful, and multiply, and replenish the earth, and subdue it; and have dominion over the fish of the sea, and over the birds of the sky, and over every living thing that creeps upon the earth." And God said: "Behold, I have given you every seed-bearing plant, which is upon the face of all the earth, and every tree that has seed-bearing fruit—they shall be yours for food; and to every animal of the earth, and to every bird of the sky, and to every thing that creeps upon the earth, wherein there is a living soul, I have given every green herb for food." And it was so. And God saw every thing that God had made, and, behold, it was very good. And there was evening and there was morning, the sixth day.

Genesis 1:26–31

Stamped in God's Image

"Who am I?" and "Does my life here have meaning and purpose?" are questions that some among us often ask. In pondering these questions I frequently turn to the creation accounts in the opening chapters of the Book of Genesis. "Then God said: 'Let us make man in our image, after our likeness' . . . God created man in His image; in the divine image He created him; male and female He created them . . . God looked at everything He had made, and he found it very good" (Genesis 1:26–31).

It is so easy to see the negative and the bad in myself and others, and to stop there. But these lines of Genesis challenge me to see the whole picture. They move me to discover the divine image in myself, to know and acknowledge my goodness. They also remind me that every person I meet each day bears the divine image and is also filled with goodness.

Chapters two and three of Genesis describe God's love for Adam and Eve and His desire for an intimate and loving relationship with them. It is in such a relationship with God and all others in my life that I come to know the image of God with which I am stamped, and in these relationships I also come to know more fully why God looks upon me, the person He created, and says that I am "very good."

Bishop Gerald Wilkerson is an Auxiliary Bishop for the Archdiocese of Los Angeles and the Regional Bishop for the San Fernando Pastoral Region (the San Fernando, Santa Clarita and Antelope Valleys). He oversees the pastoral work of the Catholic Church and the nearly one hundred priests who serve nearly one million Catholics in the fifty-five parishes and elementary schools, twelve Catholic high schools, three Catholic hospitals, and two Catholic cemeteries in the region. He served as pastor of Our Lady of Grace Parish in Encino, California from 1982 until 1997 when he was named a Bishop by Pope John Paul II.

B'tzelem Elohim—In God's Image

The story is told that once the Baal Shem Tov (Besht) summoned Sammael, the Lord of demons, because of some important matter that he wished to command Sammael to do, but Sammael resisted. So the Besht told his disciples to bare their foreheads to Sammael, and, on every forehead, the Lord of demons saw inscribed the sign of the image in which God creates the human being—*b'tzelem Elohim*—"in God's image."

Sammael was disarmed, and then agreed to do the Besht's bidding, but asked humbly and beseechingly before departing, "Oh Sons of the living God, permit me to stay here just a little longer and gaze upon your foreheads" (*Tales of the Hasidim: Book One*, Martin Buber).

In my life and work I encounter people every day, some wonderful with open hearts and pure souls, and some challenging, self-centered and mean-spirited. This story and Genesis 1:26–27 is, in most circumstances, my "default verse of Torah," the one that reminds me who I am, who we all are and before Whom we all stand.

When those standing before me are pure and sweet souls, I see the words *b'tzelem Elohim* flowing from their every pore. When they are not so wondrous, I search for the sign of God on their foreheads and imagine what kind of world we would have if each one of us looked for that sign in everyone we meet.

Rabbi John L. Rosove is the Senior Rabbi of Temple Israel of Hollywood, Los Angeles.

Tzelem Elohim: Recognizing the Godly within Ourselves and Others

Every member of the human race is a recipient of being created "in the image of God." In later generations, the rabbis affirmed this principle, remarking that every human being is distinctive, yet all are in God's image.

As a rabbi, I come across the entire range of human behavior. Rabbis (as well as clergy of other communities of faith) see the best and the worst that humanity can exhibit. It is easy for me to categorize people as good or bad, to dismiss those whose behaviors I find repulsive or to almost deify those whose behavior seems the epitome of righteousness.

The idea that all humanity is created *b'tzelem Elohim*, in God's image, helps me each day to balance my perspective about the people I come into contact with. The student who gives me a hard time, the congregant who has committed a crime, the colleague who is difficult to work with, are all created in God's image as much as the neighbor who each week serves meals at the homeless shelter or the friend who donates generously to every noble cause.

The influences that cause one human being to hide his/her Godly characteristics or cause another to shine are complex, no doubt. But whenever a person enters my office or classroom, I rise before them, as I remind myself that s/he represents the image of God, and therefore deserves my respect and honor.

At the same time, I ask that those with whom I interact acknowledge that spark of divinity within me. Like everyone, I live in the "real" world, having mundane business to conduct and everyday conversations and relationships. And yet there is a part of me, always playing in the background (at least) that is Godly. When others speak to my higher self, that *tzelem Elohim* (divine image) in me, it raises me and our relationship to a higher level.

And that, in turn, elevates both of us as well as anyone else with whom we will come into contact.

Rabbi Arnold D. Samlan is Founder and President of Jewish Connectivity, a Jewish Life Coaching and Consulting practice. He is also a staff member of the New Center for Collaborative Leadership at The Jewish Education Project. A native of Chicago, he has served in many settings as a Jewish educational leader. His workshops and classes for teachers, adults and teens, offered throughout the United States and Israel, have garnered rave reviews. His writings have appeared in several journals, as well as in his blog, The Notorious R.A.V.

All God's Children

The biblical verse that has most impacted my life is Genesis 1:27. It is repeated similarly in Genesis 5:1. This verse was emphasized by my teacher Rabbi Yitz Greenberg, and by Ben Azai in the Talmud as the most important verse in all of the Torah.

This verse has always spoken to my soul, to the G-d within, to my intuitive swift grasp of truth. I have always felt G-d's spirit in this created life. When I look at the complexity of the human condition, the uniqueness of each human life, the capacity to achieve extraordinary accomplishments from the construction of huge skyscrapers to minute computers, from the beauty and majesty of nature to my own inquiring mind searching for meaning. I know that within the grandeur and the mystery is the Holy Spirit, my intimate partner, the Force that stands behind it (and within me) and that compels me to follow the implications of the verse that every human being is created in the image of G-d.

I have found my own particular calling from this verse and that is my passion to help every human being become the very one s/he is meant to be, to help each person reach his or her potential, to treat each person with respect and to try to be as open and present with them as I can possibly be.

I believe that all the details of the Torah are an elaboration of this central idea, an attempt to concretize in every aspect of life the values that follow from the fact that every human being is created in the image of G-d. Thus I believe to work to remove injustice in the world, to support the hungry in body and spirit, to be responsible to our own gifts and actualize our blessed destinies in this world are mandates that follow this exalted verse in our time-limited existence. The verse is universal in nature, suggesting, as Abraham Joshua Heschel captured, "that G-d is either the G-d of every human being, or the G-d of no human being."

Moreover, as I look at other verses in the Torah that may present challenges to me as a person living in the 21st century, I always weigh them in the light of this primal verse; and if I encounter certain traditions or values that have arisen in my community due to fear (that contradict this primary value), I turn to this verse as a guide to my response and my soul knows its truth.

Rabbi Mel Gottlieb, Ph.D., is President of the Academy for Jewish Religion, California. He was ordained from Yeshiva University and holds a Ph.D. in Depth Psychology/Mythology from Pacifica Graduate Institute. Rabbi Gottlieb has been on the faculty of Yeshiva University, Columbia University, USC School of Social Work, and Pacifica Graduate Institute teaching psychology and religion and has published in various journals articles on *Mussar*, Kabbalah, and Jungian Psychology. Rabbi Gottlieb has been a psychotherapist in private practice over twenty years, former Hillel Director at M.I.T. and Princeton, and a pulpit rabbi in several congregations in Los Angeles.

On Human Dignity

In the play *A Man for All Seasons*, Sir Thomas More, speaking to his daughter Margaret, has this to say: "God made the angels to show His splendor, as He made the animals for their innocence and plants for their simplicity. But man He made to serve Him wittily in the tangle of his mind."

I have always believed that our greatest downfall is to miss who we truly are as beloved creatures of God! If I would get something for every time I have felt less than what I am, limited, depressed, lacking in confidence, etc., I would probably be a very wealthy man by now. I believe this is true of many, if not all human beings. Therefore a constant reminder of our human dignity is of key importance in being able to wake up every morning with a sense of purpose in life. This is what, in the words of Archbishop Fulton Sheen, makes us wake up every morning and say, "Good morning, God!" instead of "Good God, morning!"

These verses of Genesis remind me that we are called to be partners of God, partners with each other in the same dignity we have received from God. These verses that proclaim our human dignity in God should be part of every creed we profess. It should be an article of every faith!

These verses are a constant reminder of who we are: neither gods nor beasts. When we try to be like God we lose ourselves; when we downgrade ourselves imitating beast-like behavior, we no longer recognize that we are to be our brothers' and sisters' keepers. These verses remind us of our dignity and our place in the world and in relation to each other. No other truth has offered me a better paradigm to understand at all times, in all places, in my relationship with a loving God and with all peoples, how to live my life to the fullest.

Very Reverend José I. Lavastida, M.A. (Notre Dame Seminary), S.T.L., S.T.D. (Accademia Alfonsiana, Rome, Italy), is President Rector and Full Professor of Theology at Notre Dame Seminary. He has a doctorate in Moral Theology from the Alfonsian Academy in Rome, an Institute of Moral Theology of the Lateran University. He has a concentration in bioethics and his doctoral dissertation was published under the title "Health Care and the Common Good." Father Lavastida is also a novelist with his first novel entitled *Better for One Man to Die*, based on the life and ministry of St. Anthony Marie Claret in Cuba. Fr. Lavastida is Cuban-born, a U.S. citizen since 1974, and a Chaplain and Lieutenant Commander in the U.S. Navy, serving with distinction in Iraq and receiving the Presidential Unit Citation from the President of the United States in 2003. He served as Academic Dean of the Seminary for nine years and has served as President Rector since July 31, 2007.

No Longer Second Rate
Genesis 1:27

When I was ten years old I decided to read the entire Bible. I don't remember now how far I got in this project, but I do remember that the experience brought me closer to God and formed the basis for the faith I have had ever after.

The creation stories spoke to my imagination and filled me with wonder. At the time I didn't realize that there were two separate accounts of creation; that insight would come many years later. For most of my early years I accepted the view that women and girls were second class citizens and inferior to men.

Wasn't Eve the reason humans were banished from the garden? Wasn't she an afterthought, anyway, created to be a wife/stay-at-home mother/helpmate to her husband Adam? When I was growing up in the 1940s and '50s I never met a female doctor, clergyperson, or business owner. The films I saw and the TV programs I watched then showed women acting silly and spending their energies looking for a husband. Even when I was in college my teachers encouraged me to think of my liberal arts education as an asset for my husband and for my future volunteer activities.

The dawning women's movement of the 1960s and '70s changed my views and changed my life. Through the writings of female scholars and through a new generation of teachers (I was in graduate school then), I saw my place in the world differently. I saw that in God's eyes women were on the same level with men. I was created in God's image just as surely as a man was. Even though the world at large had not adopted this view yet, it gave me courage to pursue my dreams and to realize my potential.

My denomination first ordained women clergy in 1977. Right away I began my journey towards the ordained ministry. It took ten years to reach that goal, as there were many obstacles to overcome. A primary one was my bishop who said he couldn't ordain me because "I can't find jobs for women clergy." I had to move to another diocese (with my husband and two children) in order to find a bishop who would welcome me. Even after I was ordained and serving a congregation, I continued to run into people who thought I was second-rate because I was a woman.

My first post was ministering to two small rural parishes, a hard to fill position because there had been "trouble" there. The first week I was on the job I called on a vestryman, a doctor, and I asked him how he felt about having a woman priest. "Beggars can't be choosers," he replied.

His feelings were not unique, I discovered. What sustained me during those early years of ministry was my belief that I was called to this work and that God approved.

Nancy Bloomer is a retired Episcopal priest and college teacher of literature and writing. She lives in Vermont.

God's Divine Love

The creation story in the First Book of Moses (Genesis chapters 1 and 2) contains the profound basis for my faith and spirituality. After God created the world and all living things, God saw that it was good. The pinnacle of creation is humanity which God created in His own image and animated with His very breath and spirit (*ruach*). The significance of these concepts is the foundation for mainline Christian theology and spirituality.

First, what God created was good. This means that the world and our humanity is not relegated to a degraded and even evil substance which we must somehow strive to overcome. On the contrary, God's creation is fundamentally good and although we sometimes stray from being all we were created to be, we are not debased creatures. Second, humanity is created in the image of God and, furthermore, is actually enlivened with the very spirit of God. This means that our Creator is very personal to us, and we are not radically separated from God. There have been interpretations of Christianity throughout history up to the present which consider the physical condition substantially evil which must be overcome through mortification. This finds expression in various forms of sectarian Christianity up to the present day.

Accepting the goodness of creation and the intrinsic connection of the human condition to God is the substance for the most important Christian belief, namely the incarnation. This primary point of Christian faith maintains that because the created world, including humanity, is so good God actually embraced the physical by becoming one of us (in the person of Jesus of Nazareth), bringing us even closer to our Source by this supreme act of Divine love. My personal faith is framed by this belief.

The Reverend Mark D. Stuart is an Episcopal priest in the Diocese of Los Angeles. Having been in the ordained ministry for over thirty years, Stuart has served in a variety of positions both as a parish priest and as executive director for Episcopal social service agencies across the United States. Most recently, he served the parish of St. Thomas the Apostle, Hollywood, as Associate Rector for Parish Growth and Development and currently serves the Diocese of Los Angeles in the role of parish interim and transitional ministry capacities.

The Very Good of Creation—Genesis 1:31

Every Friday night Jewish people make a blessing over wine to sanctify Shabbat. The liturgy begins with the announcement of Shabbat at the end of the Torah's first creation story: "the sixth day, and the heavens and the earth were completed and all their host. And God completed in the seventh day the work that the

One had made . . . and rested . . . and blessed . . . and made it holy. . . ." Every week when I celebrate Shabbat, I add to the liturgy the verse that comes before this: "And God saw everything the One had made and behold: it is very good!" (Genesis 1:31). This declaration is the climax of the whole Creation story, and its importance was recognized by generations of commentators, Jewish and Christian. It tells us that nothing is more important than Creation itself. Without this seeing, there can be no Shabbat, no sense of completion. Shabbat, the day of rest, is the center of gravity for all Jewish rituals, the only ritual in the Ten Commandments, and Creation—the holiness, wholeness, and beauty of Creation—is the focal point of Shabbat.

What is it then that makes Creation very good? We think we know what is good, that is, good for us, but the early rabbis said that what makes Creation "very" is: the evil inclination, the angel of death, and death itself. Those very things that undo what seems best to us are what make this universe so blessed. I hear in this interpretation an affirmation of so much, including the essentiality of evolution—that is, the process of birth and death that leads to change in species—for the growth and fulfillment of Creation.

Maimonides (renowned Torah scholar of the Middle Ages) interpreted this verse to mean, "the individuals of the human species and all the more so the other species, are things of no value in comparison with the whole that exists and endures." This is a humbling perspective, and one that is fundamental to my work on ecotheology. But there is another perspective on my mind every Friday night when I make the blessing. Though it is sweet to remember the good things that happened in the week leading up to Shabbat, I also try to recall the hard things—the disappointments, hurts, and fears—and to remember that these too are very good. And sometimes, when my vision is just right, I can see in my heart what it means to say that even, especially, death is good.

Rabbi David Seidenberg is a theologian, dancer, and activist who teaches eco-Torah and *nigunim* (Jewish spirituals) through his website, www.neohasid.org. He was ordained both by the Jewish Theological Seminary in New York City and by Rabbi Zalman Schachter-Shalomi and wrote a doctorate on ecology and Kabbalah. David lives in Northampton, Massachusetts and teaches throughout North America and the world.

And God blessed the seventh day, and made it holy;
because in it God rested from all the work which God in
creating had made.

Genesis 2:3

And God Rested

What a challenge to pick one verse out of all the others! This
verse from Genesis is my choice. It is not my choice because of
the wonder of creation or the Sabbath but because it says that
God rested.

As a pastor, my world is a world full of deadlines, schedules,
study, services, counseling, meetings, visiting the sick and a mul-
titude of administrative details. Communicating through email,
voice mail, snail mail and phone calls are the normal fabric of
any given day. There are many moments of pressure ranging
from minor to significant. My world is hardly much different
from that of others, specifically in my "busyness." And it is in
my busyness that I receive compliments, encouragement and
satisfaction. Even though there are moments of prayer, it is
about my busyness that I talk. Ask me how my day went—I will
talk about my busyness.

And God rested! We gravitate to thanking and praising God
for His six days of creation and I do that. But most of all HE
RESTED!

I love that the author told us that. It is my permission to
stop, to listen and to sip coffee. In a world that is purpose-
driven, goal-oriented and managed by objective, it is my permission
to "waste time" with children in the parking lot and to hit a little
white ball among trees and fairways. It is my permission to get
off the merry-go-round and bask in wonder at the results of the
six days of creation. He poured His energy into creation and

then rested. I enjoy creation, suck energy out of it, and I rest. In a world where "doing" is valued more than "being," I rest. The Almighty Being, the great "I AM," HE RESTED.

Monsignor Robert McNamara was ordained a priest in Ireland in 1969. He has spent forty-two years serving in seven different parishes in Los Angeles and is presently pastor at St. Bernardine of Siena in Woodland Hills, California.

And there went up a mist from the earth, and watered the whole face of the ground. And the Eternal One God formed man of the dust of the ground, and breathed into his nostrils the breath of life; and man became a living soul. And the Eternal One God planted a garden eastward, in Eden; and there God put the man whom God had formed.

Genesis 2:6–8

God's Touch

In her poem, "The Summer Day," Pulitzer Prize winner Mary Oliver begins by asking the question "Who made the world?" More than simply asking a rhetorical question, the faith-filled poet seems to stand in wonder and awe as she continues to contemplate God's creatures and all creation.

"God looked at everything He had made, and He found it very good." This blessing of God upon His work found in the first chapter of Genesis has always and hopefully will continue to inform my ministry as an artist and priest.

As a young boy, I vividly remember my mother or father asking me on occasion—with some frustration—"Do you have to touch everything?" I thought it was an odd question, and I simply continued to hone what would become my most developed and valued sense. When I first discovered the creation stories in a huge illustrated Bible we kept on the coffee table in the living room, I was captivated by the telling of the second and earlier creation narratives; it seemed to me that God Himself had to touch everything!

In verse six of the second chapter of Genesis, we read, "but a stream was welling up out of the earth and was watering all the surface of the ground." Approaching the sacred scriptures as an aging adult, what I grasped as a child remains largely intact. Through still stunning metaphors of sculptor, gardener, and lover of life, I too stand in awe with the poet; this God is so close to the earth—working and playing with it . . . even closer to His people, He shares His very breath with them and me.

The waters of creativity continue to well up from the depths of who I am as a child of God. Introduced to my faith through the symbolic dying and rising in the waters of Baptism, I continue as both priest and artist to celebrate the sacramental revelation of God.

Father Bill Moore SS.CC. (Latin initials for Sacred Hearts) is a member of the Congregation of the Sacred Hearts of Jesus and Mary, also known as the Picpus Fathers. The first and only member of his order to major in art, he graduated in 1972 from St. Mary's University, Winona, Minnesota. Fr. Bill received a Master of Divinity from the Washington Theological Coalition in Silver Spring, Maryland, and was ordained in Glendora, California. He has taught high school art and religious studies. Following fifteen years of ministry in education, he served nine years as both associate pastor and pastor at Holy Name of Mary Church in San Dimas, California. In 1998, he was assigned to work full-time as a professional artist and believes "we need to slow down, look, explore and consider the essential colors, shapes and textures that can feed our souls." All proceeds from the sale of his art are given to his religious order.

And the Eternal One God said: "It is not good that the man should be alone; I will make a fitting helper for him."

Genesis 2:18

What Love Is

In my last year of rabbinical school I accompanied my rabbi to a *shiva minyan*. It was the final day of the week of mourning for a beautiful and humble man who had suffered terribly from a debilitating illness. His daughter, who had spent every day for several years lovingly cleaning, feeding and caring for him, was the primary mourner. She was grief-stricken. Her apartment had been transformed into a capacious tribute to his memory, lined with photographs and handwritten letters. After reciting *Mourner's Kaddish*, my rabbi picked up a photo of the woman's father. He handed it to her and said, "Say goodbye to your father. Right now—in front of all these people. He is dead. But *you*— *you* are alive." She cried out in anguish and held the photo against her chest. I was horrified by his forcefulness, his abruptness. For several minutes we sat in excruciating silence, witnesses to her brokenheartedness. But finally she stood, looked deeply into her father's eyes in the photo, and said goodbye. Then we all got up and walked around the block— signifying the end of the most acute stage of grieving—and sang a sad but hopeful Halleluyah.

I learned that morning a bit about what love is.

Our Rabbis teach that when God created Eve to be Adam's *ezer k'negdo*—helpmate—it was to help him by OPPOSING him. Eve was to be his *hevruta*, his sparring partner. Her purpose was to push him beyond what he was comfortable with, what he would naturally come to on his own. *Lo tov heyot adam levado*—it's not good for a person to be alone, because Jews live dialogically—

we argue, we interact, we wrestle. The job of one partner is to help refine and strengthen and hone the other, not through acquiescence, but through loving challenge. Rabbi Yohanan and Resh Lakish were lifelong *hevruta* in the Talmud. For each point that Rabbi Yohanan would make, Resh Lakish would offer twenty-four challenges. To each of those challenges, Rabbi Yohanan would give twenty-four answers, until the truth would become clear to both of them (*Bava Metzia* 84a). Truth emerges through rigorous, loving encounter.

Somehow, through his willingness to touch her deepest pain, my rabbi dared to give that mourner her life back.

I learned that morning that love is the willingness to speak exactly the truth the other needs to hear to begin to heal. And love is the willingness to hear it. It could be a partner, a friend, a rabbi, a therapist—someone willing to shine a light into your heart and speak truth to you. The Talmud teaches that a person cannot free herself from prison (*Brakhot* 5b). Love is about letting someone help break you free.

Rabbi Sharon Brous is the founding rabbi of IKAR, a spiritual community dedicated to reanimating Jewish life through soulful religious practice that is rooted in a deep commitment to social justice (www.ikar-la.org). She lives in Los Angeles with her husband, David, and their three children—Eva, Sami, and Levi.

And the man said: "This is now bone of my bones, and flesh of my flesh; she will be called Woman, because she was taken out of Man." <u>Therefore</u> will a man leave his father and his mother, and will cleave to his wife, and they will be as one flesh.

Genesis 2:23–24

"Therefore"

The evening *Ma'ariv* prayer that precedes the *Sh'ma* speaks of God's love of the House of Israel, and of the Torah, law, and precept, which God has taught His people. The prayer continues with an easily overlooked word, but one which captures human moral responsibility. That word is "therefore"—in Hebrew, *al ken*. The same word appears in the *Aleinu* prayer, at the close of the service, preceding the recitation of the *Mourner's Kaddish*.

The "therefore" in prayer calls my attention to the "therefore" in the Bible's human-divine relationship. "Therefore" calls upon the co-signers of the covenant to turn belief into behavior, to verify the oaths and to act out the resolution of the dialogue. "Therefore" is the hinge upon which the door between God and Israel swings open.

Implicitly and explicitly, the "therefore" of consequences is the subterranean stream beneath the biblical narrative. We come upon it in the Bible, early. "Therefore—*al ken*—a man leaves his father and mother and clings to his wife, so that they become as of one flesh" (Genesis 2:24). The incestuous ties must be broken before the marital union can be realized.

"Therefore" lies at the edge of conscience: To believe or not to believe, what does it matter? To petition or not to petition, who is it that is called upon to intervene, and what have I to do with the need to intervene, to put my body between the sword of the predator and the hunted victim? To petition or not to petition; what difference does it make whether I rely upon the inscrutable will of God or I take action myself?

God is known in the Bible as the liberator of the slaves of Egypt. Is that a claim of divine power, or does it call me to free the tortured pariahs from the dark dungeons of enslavement?

"Therefore" usually comes toward the end of the meeting, toward the conclusion of the conference, toward the last psalm of the prayer book. "Therefore" follows me from the synagogue into my home, and from my home into the marketplace. It is the haunting question beneath the rhetoric of law and lore. Without "therefore," prayer and scripture are changeless words. Without "therefore," the words remain the same, the world remains the same, I remain the same.

Rabbi Harold M. Schulweis has been the spiritual leader of Valley Beth Shalom in Encino, California, since 1970. He has authored numerous books including the award-winning *Conscience: The Duty to Obey and the Duty to Disobey*. Rabbi Schulweis is the founding chairman of the Jewish Foundation for the Righteous which identifies and offers grants to those non-Jews who risked their lives to save Jews during the Holocaust. In 2004, he founded the Jewish World Watch dedicated to raising awareness and funds to protest genocide and assist victims of its unrest.

Loving Down Deep in Our Bones

These two verses from the second creation story are the ones that have grabbed me as the years have gone on. The Yahwist writer has great insight into the depth of relationships which moves me as I have met with hundreds of opposite gender and same gender couples to create together their marriage ceremonies. I meet with couples for a year to provide support and so that I can hear them as they understand who they are individually and what it means to dare to love another.

I change some of the wording of the text not to dishonor it but to truly acknowledge the assumptions of the writer's day. "Then the man said, 'This at last is bone of my bones and flesh of my flesh, this one is named woman.' Therefore a man leaves his father and mother supported by community and goes to his beloved and a woman leaves her father and mother supported by community and goes to her beloved creating their chosen family and they become one flesh."

My love of this text and emphasis is always, "This at last is bone of my bones and flesh of my flesh." To love someone from deep in your bones carries with it a knowledge and trust of such profound meaning. I am reminded of the great Jewish theologian Martin Buber who wrote that every particular I-Thou relationship is a glimpse into the Eternal Thou who is God. And a wonderful Catholic priest I met in Washington, DC many years ago said, "God is that which happens between you and me." It is this kind of mutual knowing, respect and love that is called forth in loving another. I want for couples, regardless of sexual orientation, a healthy, loving, mutual relationship supported by community, family, and a faith tradition (if they so choose). I believe our spiritual practices, faith communities and religious/spiritual leaders can nurture couples as they grow throughout their lives together. Spiritual/religious leaders and communities of faith/spiritual practice have a responsibility to help create a safe place for couples to grow as they create their own histories and herstories, which are all a part of God's story.

This deep to the bone loving moves us more authentically and intimately into a creative partnership with God calling us into a maturity of adulthood where sexuality and spirituality become friends integrated into our very beings. I believe this Yahwist writer understands well that this kind of deep to the bone loving is a part of healing our world as well.

Reverend Dr. Jane Adams Spahr ("Janie") is a twin sister, a mother of two wonderful sons, grandmother of one amazing grand-daughter (Riley) and one amazing grandson (Elliott), partner of a beloved one, wife emerita of her former husband, friend, lesbian feminist, a learner and teacher and retired Presbyterian minister. She was a pastor of churches in Pittsburgh, San Francisco, and San Rafael, California. She was founding Executive Director of Spectrum Center of LGBT Concerns for ten years in San Anselmo, California, and Minister Director of That All May Freely Serve for seventeen years centered in the Downtown United Presbyterian Church in Rochester, New York.

And they were both naked, the man and his wife, and were not ashamed.

Genesis 2:25

What Does God Think of Me?

The verse that is meaningful to me might be surprising, but it is Genesis 2:25, "And the man and the woman were both naked and were not ashamed."

You might ask, "Why is a Catholic priest who is celibate and not married picking this verse?" It has to do with my love of John Paul II's *Theology of the Body*. John Paul II looks at this scripture from the viewpoint of what it must have been like for us before sin. How did we experience our bodies before sin?

We live in an age that sees the spirit as good and the body as less good and, in some cases, even bad. I don't think we deliberately think this way, but it comes out in much of our thinking. Much of New Age philosophy focuses on liberating our spirits from our bodies, as if our bodies were a prison that entrapped our spirit. Remember the song from the Police, "Spirits in the Material World." This song reflects this thinking that separates the body from the soul.

This verse from Genesis is God's unconditional "Yes" to the Goodness of Our Bodies, which reveals the human person. This verse reflects what God said when He created men and women, that when He looked down upon them He saw that they were very good, that the entire person, body and soul, is very good. Everything else was good but man and woman were very good. Anyone who has a body issue, and that would include just about everyone today, ought to reflect on this verse: that we are Very Good, not just Good but Very Good. I look at this verse as radiation for the healing of our bodies. No matter how young or old we are, how we line up with cultural norms about beauty, we can all say God made me Very Good.

Much of our culture while claiming to be pro-body actually is sending the opposite message. The world of fashion and advertising tells us that we are not good-looking enough, thin enough, that we need this product so that we can make ourselves presentable to the world.

This verse from the Book of Genesis is God telling us to stop running around and to remember that we are very good. Because we are good in our body and soul we can value ourselves and everyone we might meet. Most importantly we will know that God loves us, and we can see the goodness shine from the body in each human person.

Father Stefan Starzynski is a priest of the Diocese of Arlington, Virginia. He has been ordained for fifteen years, and he is currently serving at St. Mary of Sorrows in Fairfax, Virginia. Father Stefan is the author of the book *Miracles: Healing for a Broken World* published by Our Sunday Visitor.

And the Eternal One said to Cain: "Where is Abel, your brother?" And he said: "I do not know; am I my brother's keeper?"

Genesis 4:9

My Brother's Keeper

To me the question that Cain asks God is the most important in the Bible. The answer to that question determines everything. In my opinion both Judaism and Christianity affirm very strongly that we are the keepers of our brothers and sisters. We are all interconnected and responsible for one another. I think this is also found in Islam with its strong sense of the community. For me, religion is about helping us make sure we live up to this. This same sentiment is often expressed in the Prophets when God says in many different ways that real religion is not about offerings and worship but about caring for the widow and orphan and lifting the yoke of oppression.

Reverend Walter Cuenin is the Catholic Chaplain at Brandeis University in Waltham, Massachusetts. He also coordinates the Interfaith Chaplaincy at the university. He has been a Roman Catholic priest for forty years serving principally in the Boston area and has been active in interfaith dialogue.

And the Eternal One said to Abram: "Go forth from your land, and from your birthplace, and from your father's house, to the land that I will show you. And I will make of you a great nation, and I will bless you, and I will make your name great; and you will be a blessing. And I will bless those who bless you, and curse one that curses you; and through you will all the families of the earth be blessed." And Abram went forth, as the Eternal One had spoken to him; and Lot went with him; and Abram was seventy-five years old when he went out from Haran.

Genesis 12:1–4

Rooted and Free

In many ways, the call that came to Abram and Sarai—*go forth on a journey*—is a call that we all hear. But there are a few differences. For one thing, a woman is no longer an appendage to a man; the partners in a relationship often have different, even opposing, calls and passions. And our calls can be less straightforward. What does it mean to go forth?

I think of a friend, a woman rabbi, who moved across the country to take a position as a senior rabbi. She left one strong congregation for another, her family left one beautiful home for another. But her journey also began with some of the uncertainty of Abram and Sarai. There was a smidgen of barrenness in the forces that propelled her. She knew her journey would involve deep loss.

What makes the journey really tough is getting pulled up by the roots, after building relationships and networks. It's tough on kids, too, which is why most folks stay put, if possible, once kids are in middle school.

I think of the gorgeous hydrangea plant in our backyard. It has these gorgeous blue flowers; the only problem, it's behind the garage and you can't see it. I asked my friend, Kris Culp, a theologian and a good gardener, "Could I dig it up? Move it?" She said, "I don't know, after five or six years, the roots go pretty deep. If you are going to move it, do it in the spring, before it's started any leaf development. If you wait until it's flowering, it's really hard to uproot."

The call to *go forth* sometimes causes us to uproot. In his book, *Falling Upward: A Spirituality for the Two Halves of Life*, Father Richard Rohr writes that sooner or later in the spiritual life, "some event, person, death, idea, or relationship will enter your life that you simply cannot deal with, using your present skill set, your acquired knowledge, or your strong will-power. . . . You will stumble over a necessary stumbling stone, as Isaiah calls it." He says that dealing with this kind of loss or challenge can become an experience of "falling upward," providing an opportunity to give back fully and freely what was first given to us!

When we are called to *go forth*, we go trusting the One who calls us, trusting that as we go to the deepest part of ourselves and in the deep love of God, our call will contribute to the blossoming, the flourishing of God's good creation.

Reverend Holly McKissick serves as founding pastor at Peace Christian Church (Kansas City, Missouri and Overland Park, Kansas) after twenty-one years as the founding pastor of Saint Andrew Christian Church in Olathe, Kansas. A native Texan, she was ordained at Texas Christian University's Brite Divinity School. A noted speaker and writer, Rev. McKissick and her husband, the Rev. Tom Hawley, are the parents of daughter, Eden, and son, Ben. Holly is an avid runner and enjoys marathons, gardening, cooking, reading and friends.

Letting Go
Genesis 12:1–3

Last summer I had the experience of swinging on my first ever circus trapeze. I will admit that this is something I've wanted to try ever since I saw Carrie Bradshaw and her friends do it on the television show, *Sex and the City.* I will also tell you that when the big moment arrived—standing on top of the highest ladder I've ever climbed and hanging on to a thin wooden bar—I was pretty nervous, this despite the safety net under my feet, the harness cinched around my waist, and the hands of the instructor tethering me to the platform. I am not particularly afraid of heights but still my heart pounded as I climbed the stairs, as I sailed through the air with aching arms, and as I landed in the mesh once my turn was over. But the scariest part of the experience by far? The scariest part was letting go.

I have always loved the verses of Genesis 12:1–3 because they capture not only how difficult, but also how rewarding, it can be to let go of the familiar and embrace the unknown. Abraham is asked to leave his land, his birthplace, and his father's house to set forth for a place yet unspecified, a place that God will show him. While few of us will ever have to make such complete and immediate ruptures with our past, most of us will at some point leave what is familiar to pursue a future still uncertain. It has always brought me great comfort and strength to imagine that God is with me on my life path, as God was once with Abraham, and to believe that my personal wanderings, too, will ultimately result in great blessing.

The Jewish philosopher Martin Buber wrote, "Every journey has a secret destination of which the traveler is unaware." As someone who thrives in situations of order and predictability, Abraham's story reminds me that there is only so much about our lives that we can control and encourages me to embrace the freedom, exhilaration, and possibility that come with release.

The secret destination of my own life's journey may not yet be totally apparent to me. But Abraham's story reminds me to enjoy the uncertainty of the ride!

Annie Tucker is Associate Rabbi of The Jewish Center, a Conservative congregation located in Princeton, New Jersey. A Wexner Graduate Fellow, she received both a Master's Degree in Jewish Education and rabbinic ordination from the Jewish Theological Seminary. She also holds a B.A. in Psychology and Jewish Studies from the University of Pennsylvania.

The Meaning of the Journey

Now HaShem said to Abram, "Go from your country and your kindred and your father's house to the land that I will show you. [As a consequence of your going] I will make of you a people vital to life, and I will bless you, and spread your reputation [as a people devoted to justice and compassion], so that you will be a blessing. I will bless those who bless you, and the one who curses you I will curse [those who follow the way of justice and compassion will be blessed with justice and compassion, those who do not will be cursed with injustice and cruelty]; and through you all the earth's families [human and otherwise] shall be blessed" (Genesis 12:1–3, my rendering).

This is my personal mission statement and the mission statement of the Jewish people. The Hebrew, translated here as "Go" (*lech lecha*), literally means to walk to your self, implying both an external and an internal journey. To take this journey we are challenged to leave behind nationalism, tribalism, and family baggage.

Where we are to go, the "land" mentioned here, is not articulated. This is a journey based on radical trust. We will be shown our destination only when we arrive at it. Our importance as a people depends on our taking this journey into the unknown. But the purpose of the journey is not to become great, but to become a vehicle through which all of the earth's families will be blessed.

This is why I am a Jew: Judaism challenges me to drop the known and step into the unknown. Judaism challenges me to be a blessing and a vehicle for blessing so that all life benefits from my life. While some insist Judaism is about occupying a specific piece of real estate, I think it is about embodying a specific level of consciousness: one that brings compassion and justice to all the world.

Rabbi Rami Shapiro, Ph.D., is adjunct Professor of Religion and the Director of Wisdom House, an interfaith center in Nashville. Author of over twenty books, Rami also writes a regular column for *Spirituality and Health* magazine called *Roadside Assistance for the Spiritual Traveler*. He can be reached via his website, www.rabbirami.com.

The Blessing of God's Companionship

This is one of my favorite stories in all of Scripture. In church school when I tell this story I use a sand box. I trace my hand over the sand and ponder with the children about the things in the desert that might be frightening to them—things like isolation, temperature extremes, blinding windstorms, thirst, and hunger. I talk with them about fear of the unknown or reticence to leave the comfort of a known universe. And then I tell the story of Abram whom God called from the comfort of Ur to go into the desert. In those places of isolation and fear, Abram found that God was present with him—just as He had been in Ur. The blessing that Abram received was not a life free of pain or suffering; the blessing he received was God's presence and the opportunity to live life to the fullest. Abram, or Abraham as God renamed him, was not perfect—he made terrible mistakes—but he kept plugging along. He rarely knew where or why God was calling him, but he knew at the core of his being that God had laid the foundations of the earth. He doggedly sought God's will for himself and his family, and when faced with his own human failures, he kept returning to God in faith. He knew that being in relationship with God meant stopping to offer thanks and praise as well as articulating his needs.

Life is not always easy. I have certainly had my share of deserts. I have struggled with God. But the fact that Scripture records the lives of people who struggled just as I do and yet are faithful and loved and used by God in the fulfillment of God's work—now that has given me comfort and inspiration to answer God's call. That Abram finds God in the most isolated of places gives me confidence and hope that in fact wherever I am God is right there with me in the muck. Sometimes that has led me to family and motherhood, sometimes to chaplaincy in some pretty dark places, and now to ordained ministry in a small urban parish in New England. In each place I have tried to do as Abram did—take the time to stop, build an altar, and give thanks for the blessings that God has given to me.

The Reverend Jane Bearden is the mother of three grown children, a former Clinical Laboratory Manager, and is now pastor of Trinity Episcopal Church in Haverhill, Massachusetts. She was educated at Centenary College, Mississippi State University, and Episcopal Divinity School in Cambridge, Massachusetts. She has served parishes in Lynn and Methuen, Massachusetts and Biloxi, Mississippi. She was a chaplain at Ground Zero in New York and in St. Gabriel Morgue after Hurricane Katrina.

And it came to pass in the days of Amraphel king of Shinar, Arioch king of Ellasar, Chedorlaomer king of Elam, and Tidal king of Goiim, that they made war with Bera king of Sodom, and with Birsha king of Gomorrah, Shinab king of Admah, and Shemeber king of Zeboiim, and the king of Bela which is Zoar. All these came as allies to the valley of Siddim which is the Dead Sea.

Genesis 14:1–3

And a fugitive came and told Abram the Hebrew, who was dwelling by the terebinths of Mamre the Amorite, brother of Eshcol, and brother of Aner; and these were allied with Abram. And when Abram heard that his kinsman was taken captive, he led forth his trained men, born in his house, three hundred and eighteen, and they pursued as far as Dan.

Genesis 14:13–14

And Abram said to the king of Sodom: "I have lifted up my hand to the Eternal One, God Most High, Maker of heaven and earth, that I will not take so much as a thread nor a sandal strap of that which is yours, lest you should say, 'I have made Abram rich,' only that which the young men have eaten, and the share of the men who went with me, Aner, Eshkol, and Mamre, let them take their share."

Genesis 14: 22–24

Genesis 14: A Fugitive Message

Since my bar mitzvah, the weekly reading *Lekh Lekha* (Genesis chapters 12–17) has been meaningful to me. Over the years I have come to appreciate its significance, but that was not so when I was thirteen years old. Nevertheless, I did appreciate one section, chapter 14, the battle of four kings against five. It is dramatic, almost cinematographic in places. Abram, the hero, plays a role that a young person can relate to. While most of the rest of the story is somewhat obscure, it has kept me coming back over the years. In particular, I've been fascinated by "the fugitive" who arrives to inform Abram that his nephew has been taken captive. Returning to that image and what follows (Genesis 14:13–24) I have come to see that it reflects a truth about my life, and the life of the spirit in general.

I believe that our hearts and minds naturally rest in peace and ease, connected to their root in God. Yet we are easily distracted, disturbed, disappointed, dismayed. We run after desires, flee from disagreements, sit perplexed by disenchantments. War rages in us; we battle the circumstances of our lives. Our minds and hearts are taken captive all the time, and we live in confusion. We act against our own best interests, harming ourselves and others.

But, when we are able to pause for a minute—perhaps in the company of confederates or allies, teachers, fellow congregants, God—we make ourselves open to the arrival of "the fugitive." Our deepest desire, our true self, calls out to us: "Your life has been taken captive." In that moment we are invited to pay attention, to notice what is true, and to gather our "retainers"—collecting our thoughts, reviving our mindfulness. In that moment we can reclaim what is truly important: faithfulness, honesty, love, compassion, justice. We can reconnect with our true selves. We ask no reward of anyone in that moment, as we rest in the peace and ease of the God within and without.

This has been my experience. I sense that the "fugitive" is always arriving, with each breath, in each moment, inviting me to reclaim the deep connection to God that has been taken captive in the endless conflicts and confusions of daily living. All I have to do in that moment is bring myself home.

Rabbi Jonathan P. Slater was ordained at the Jewish Theological Seminary of America and has a Doctor of Ministry degree from the Pacific School of Religion. He is author of *Mindful Jewish Living: Compassionate Practice* and Co-Director of Programs of The Institute for Jewish Spirituality, as well as instructor in meditation at the JCC in Manhattan and in other venues.

". . . Far be it from You to do this thing, to slay the right-eous with the wicked, as if the righteous were as the wicked; far be it from You; should not the judge of all the earth do justly?"

Genesis 18:25

A God We Can Argue With

In the 1991 film *The Quarrel*, two Holocaust survivors—friends from the old country—meet by chance after the war. One of them has become much *more* religious because of what he en-dured, while the other has become an atheist. Here are all the great questions: What use is a God who lets evil run rampant? The atheist character is furious with God! But does it make sense to be furious with a God you don't believe in?

It was Abraham who discovered a God we can be angry with, argue with, discuss with. Abraham was shocked by God's willingness to destroy the wicked city of Sodom, though there must have been *some* righteous people there. He cried out: "Shall not the judge of all the earth do justice?" This is why we love Abraham, and why we love God: because our relationship with the Deity is about dialogue and debate; because God created the world incomplete so that we might participate in perfecting it. And as each of us is created in the Divine image (Genesis 1:27), each has a distinctive role to play in the cosmic drama. The *Mishnah* compares God's creation of humanity to a mint that improbably stamps out coins of which no two are alike (*Sanhedrin* 4:5).

Why is God so hard to find? God is famously absent from the Book of Esther, but the rabbis make a pun on *Esther* and *hester*, Hebrew for "hiding" (Talmud *Chullin* 139b). God is hid-den in this story but present for those who truly need God: the book's miraculous reversal of fortune makes that clear. We are meant to keep searching for God, especially in times of crisis, and to use Abraham's technique of challenge and outrage to move our quest forward.

Rabbi Joe Hample grew up in New York, worked for many years as a systems analyst at Wells Fargo Bank in San Francisco, and was ordained at Hebrew Union College in Los Angeles in 2009. He lives with his husband Barry Wendell in Crescent City, California and serves as the Jewish Chaplain at Pelican Bay State Prison.

And when the Eternal One finished speaking to Abraham,
God departed; and Abraham returned to his place.

Genesis 18:33

Encountering God

On March 23, 1973 I stood in the delivery room for the birth of
my son. For various reasons, that had not been possible when
his older sisters were born. As I watched Adam arrive, and
heard his lusty cry, I felt a surge of emotions: relief, certainly,
and instant love, but also gratitude and awe, a sense of transcendent closeness to the Source of life. I hasten to add that my
love for and amazement at being the father of Jo-Ellen and
Naomi is no less great. But this time I was in the middle of the
action.

I reflect on those feelings often, reminded of the closing
words of the debate between God and Abraham over the de-
struction of Sodom and Gomorrah: "The Eternal departed
when He finished speaking to Abraham, and Abraham returned
to his place" (Genesis 18:33). In a critical moment, the patriarch
found a transcendent closeness to God; he was elevated to a
sphere of spiritual existence beyond physical space and time.
But "God left . . . and Abraham returned to his place." The in-
tensity of the encounter was fleeting. Its echo must have been at
the very core of Abraham's being.

Over the years of my rabbinate, I confess I have at times
been challenged by doubt: death or illness or tragedy have
seemed unfair and unjust. Seeking to comfort those who suffer, I have been hard-pressed to find meaning in the moment,
and so, shaken in my own belief. Faced with that uncertainty,
with more questions than answers, I return always to the instant when I saw new life enter the world. When I despair of

encountering God, I remember when I did; and knowing that it is possible is enough.

Lewis C. Littman is Rabbi Emeritus at Temple Bat Yam, Fort Lauderdale, Florida.

And God said: "Take now your son, your only son, who you love, Isaac, and go out to the land of Moriah; and offer him there for a burnt-offering upon one of the mountains of which I will tell you." And Abraham rose early in the morning, and saddled his ass, and took two of his young men with him, and Isaac his son; and he cleaved the wood for the burnt-offering, and he rose up, and he went to the place of which God had told him.

Genesis 22:2–3

The Urgency of Obedience

Genesis 22 is a powerful story in which Abraham is told to sacrifice his son as a burnt offering. At first glance it is very easy to miss an important word in the text. After God gave Abraham the instructions, the text says Abraham got up *early* to do it. Aren't there other options other than complete obedience?

Couldn't he say, "No, he is indeed the one I love, so sacrificing him as a burnt offering is out of the question." Or maybe Abraham should get his wife's opinion! Surely she would not allow him to sacrifice their son. Another possible option is to weigh the pros and cons and make the best decision possible. Well, Abraham does none of that. He simply obeys.

But do you remember that important word I mentioned? He got up *early* to do it. I only get up early to do things I really look forward to doing. Meeting a friend for breakfast? Easy. I'll get up early for that. Leaving for vacation? Oh, even easier, and I don't even need an alarm clock. Sacrificing my son? Excuse me? That's not on my list of things that would get me up at the crack of dawn. But it was for Abraham.

I believe what got Abraham up though was his desire to obey God. Abraham even chose to obey the things he didn't fully understand. He had no idea what God's plan was with all of this. He just obeyed without knowing the rest of the story. Today we pick and choose what to obey, and if we don't fully understand, or if it does not make sense, we're not budging! In Abraham's powerful story, we don't see the questioning of obedience—we see the urgency of obedience. And he saw the mighty power of God.

The story is a wonderful reminder to me, a reminder that God loves me and wants His best for me. Living in a broken world, it's easy to think we know best. We want our things in our time, in our way. I lived many years of my life that way. Abraham teaches me that God *always* knows best and I am wise to obey . . . even when I don't fully understand.

Henry J. Rogers is an ordained Baptist pastor and serves as the corporate chaplain for Interstate Batteries, located in Dallas, where he has served for the past twenty years.

And when she had finished giving him drink, she said: "I will draw for your camels also, until they have finished drinking." And she hurried, and she emptied her pitcher into the trough, and she ran again to the well to draw, and drew for all his camels.

Genesis 24:19–20

Embracing Life

I have always loved the compassion and eagerness of Rebecca. She has a life-giving spirit, a spirit of adventure and trust. To this point in Genesis we have not seen positive views of women. Sarah and Hagar were known for their animosity. Sarah laughed in disbelief when she heard that she would bear a child in her old age. Neither Sarah nor Hagar inspires us, but rather serve as catty appendages to Abraham. Lot's daughters show some initiative as they plot to become pregnant, but their actions are self-serving.

In this passage we find a woman who is her own person, kind, caring, selfless, as she hauls water for the thirsty camels of a stranger. She thinks for herself and willingly travels to a foreign land to begin a new life. As a woman I identify with Rebecca's spirit and hope, her willingness to go beyond the expected in helping those in need. My spirit dances as she embraces her unknown future. Rebecca's response from the heart stirs me from within.

I am grateful that God used Rebecca for his purposes. Rebecca could not have imagined that she would become the mother of Jacob, the grandmother of Joseph. She did not know how her life would play out; she could play it safe, but instead opened her heart to hope and new life. I could only hope that like Rebecca I would open myself to God's purpose for me with such eagerness and trust.

The Reverend Patricia O'Reilly is an Episcopal priest in the Diocese of Los Angeles, currently serving as the executive director of a social service agency assisting low-income and homeless people in Pasadena.

And they said: "Let us call to the girl, and we will ask her."
And they called to Rebeka, and said to her: "Will you go
with this man?" And she said: "I will go."

Genesis 24:57–58

Good to Go

This moment in the Book of Genesis takes my breath away. Even though Rebeka's family has already consented to her marriage to Isaac, now they are asking her whether or not she is ready to go. Their motives may be mixed—but that is irrelevant here. What matters is that the decision whether or not to leave home is left up to Rebeka. They ask her. And she answers, "I will go."

What is in that singular word of Rebeka's—*elech*—"I will go?" For me it is faith in the astonishing promise of life. Rebeka's faith frees her to take a risk, go on an adventure, trust the future, choose the unknown. Her faith is the source of her courage, the foundation of her trust.

Rebeka's word, so apparently simple yet so life-changing, has inspired me since my childhood. To my mind, it has been like a divine spark opening the door through which I could seek to embark richly and fully on my own life's journey. *Elech* has allowed me, in my life, to give up the comfort—and, at times, the comfort of the *dis*comfort—of the familiar and stride or stumble, fly or float, toward a future whose contours were at best only vaguely discernible to me.

The older I get, moreover, the more I appreciate how much Rebeka's faith has meant to me. To speak the words *I will go* with my whole being has been to overcome fear, to cherish the unpredictable, to say a resounding "Yes!" to the promise of life. It is what emboldened me as a young woman to leave the States for Israel, and then, over a decade later, to return, though I had no idea what would be in store for me. It is what has freed my mind to travel with exuberant eagerness wherever my intellectual curiosity has led me, from the poetry of William Blake to the psalms of the Bible to the prayers of the liturgy; from a passion for recipes to a love of recitative; from the world of academia to the world of the rabbinate; from climbing adventures in our national parks to skydiving in Canada.

But the greatest leap Rebeka's singular word, *elech*, freed me to take was scarcely the one out of that airplane in Canada. It was, rather, the life-changing leap I made in my 50s, saying "Yes, I will marry you," to the man I had met just weeks earlier in Cafe Moment in Jerusalem. Blessed by the faith modeled by our matriarch, I found and embraced the love of my life. And the hope I cherish today is that I am imparting that same capacity to trust, to leap, and to embrace, to my daughter.

Rabbi Miriyam Glazer is author of *Psalms of the Jewish Liturgy: A Guide to Their Beauty, Power and Meaning; Dreaming the Actual: Contemporary Fiction and Poetry by Israeli Women Writers;* and *Dancing on the Edge of the World: Jewish Stories of Faith, Inspiration and Love*, in addition to her many essays and translations. A professor of literature at American Jewish University, she has been a visiting scholar at USC, UCLA, and the Hebrew University and the recipient of major national fellowships. She is on the executive committee of the Board of Rabbis of Southern California, the advisory board of the Jewish Women's Theatre, and the editorial board of *Conservative Judaism*.

And Abraham breathed his last, and died at a good old age, an old man, and full of years; and he was gathered to his people. And Isaac and Ishmael, his sons, buried him in the cave of Machpelah, in the field of Ephron the son of Zohar the Hittite, which is before Mamre; the field which Abraham purchased from the children of Heth; there was Abraham buried, and Sarah his wife. And it came to pass after the death of Abraham, that God blessed Isaac his son; and Isaac settled near Beer-la'chai-Roi.

Genesis 25:8–11

Well of the Life-giving Vision

These words of Torah are read during *Cheshvan,* the only month of the Hebrew calendar without a special day of observance. Legend says that this month awaits its holiday. What might it be? The clue is in this text and in a modern tragedy that happened in *Cheshvan.* After Isaac's near-sacrifice at the hands of his father, Abraham, he sought comfort at *Beer-la'chai-Roi*—Well of the Life-giving Vision—a place named by Hagar, Ishmael's mother and Sarah's handmaiden, when she fled to the wilderness to escape Sarah's jealousy. Hagar discovered this well and had a vision of God.

Isaac came to this place, after Sarah's death and after the trauma of his own near-death, seeking consolation from Ishmael and Hagar—two people who had also suffered as a result of Abraham's actions. When Abraham died, the brothers buried their father. They then returned to *Beer-la'chai-Roi* to live in peace. Oh that Isaac and Ishmael could have remained there to grieve Abraham as brothers! Together they might have come to terms with the pain inflicted by their father. They would have had the opportunity to forgive each other for the obstacles to their intimate brotherly connection that were not their fault, but were the result of the decisions of their father. How different history might have been!

I believe that war is a perpetual reenactment of incompletely mourned grief. Pain is inflicted and, in response, more pain follows—it ricochets through the generations and the planet never knows peace.

This text allows me to imagine the brothers laying to rest the father who caused their suffering. It reminds me, as well, of a burial that took place in the month of *Cheshvan* in our time: that of Yitzhak Rabin. I imagine marking his *yahrzeit* with a ceremony involving descendants of Isaac and Ishmael coming together at Rabin's grave to put to rest the generations of dissension within the family. I imagine them returning to their homes, in a shared land, to live in peace. I imagine a *Yom HaShalom*, Day of Peace, rewarding the month of *Cheshvan* with its long-sought holiday, marking the sacrifices of so many of the sons of Abraham, and sealing the promise of *la'chai-Roi*, the Life-Giving Vision.

Rabbi Anne Brener, LCSW, is a psychotherapist and spiritual director, who assists institutions in creating caring communities. She is the author of the acclaimed *Mourning & Mitzvah: Walking the Mourner's Path* (Jewish Lights, 1993 & 2001) and has contributed to many other publications. She is a faculty member at the Academy for Jewish Religion, California, where she is Professor of Ritual and Human Development. Rabbi Brener is also on the faculty of Yedidya's Morei Derekh Jewish Spiritual Direction Program.

And the Eternal One appeared to him, and said: "Do not go down into Egypt; dwell in the land of which I will tell you. Live in this land, and I will be with you and I will bless you; because to you, and to your descendants, I will give all these lands, and I will establish the oath which I swore to Abraham your father. . . ."

Genesis 26:2–3

Staying out of Egypt

I never expected social justice work would be easy. But I'm not sure that I was initially prepared for the constant setbacks. Every time I turn on the computer, check my twitter feed, or open the morning paper, it seems like the world has gotten just a little more unhappy and unjust.

And so I am drawn to moments in the Torah that involve grappling with difficult circumstances.

In one such episode, a famine hits Canaan during the time of Isaac and Rebecca. God appears and commands them, *"Al tered Mitzrayma*—Do not go down to Egypt. Stay in the land which I point out to you. Reside in this land, and I will be with you and bless you" (Genesis 26:2–3).

What's so bad about going down to Egypt? If Egypt is where the food is, then why shouldn't Isaac and Rebecca bring their children there?

As we learn later in the Torah, the biblical *Mitzrayim* (Egypt) is a place that permits slavery and harsh treatment of foreigners. It is a place where the king is treated like a god and where ordinary people have little power. In descending to Egypt, Isaac and Rebecca will risk either being enslaved themselves or joining a society that condones cruelty. And by fleeing to *Mitzrayim*, the two will take care of themselves, but leave behind their starving neighbors.

Instead, God tells Isaac and Rebecca to stay put. The verb used here—*lishkon*—to dwell—indicates settling permanently, rather than just staying a while. Even in this difficult time, God insists that Isaac and Rebecca rededicate themselves to the place where they live rather than focusing only on their immediate physical needs.

I think about this command, "Don't go down to *Mitzrayim*," whenever I want to give up on justice work and to find an easier way of supporting my family. It's true that the work is frustrating and painful. But if I give up, I risk ending up in *Mitzrayim*—tolerating, or even perpetuating, injustice to those around me.

And I hold out hope for the divine blessing that this verse promises. The verb *lishkon* is also connected to the word, *Shekhina*, a name for God's caretaking presence. No matter how hard the work becomes, I try to maintain faith that if we can avoid going down to *Mitzrayim*, we can bring the *Shekhina* to dwell on earth.

Rabbi Jill Jacobs is the Executive Director of Rabbis for Human Rights–North America. She is the author of *Where Justice Dwells: A Hands-On Guide to Doing Social Justice in Your Jewish Community* (Jewish Lights, 2011) and *There Shall Be No Needy: Pursuing Social Justice Through Jewish Law and Tradition* (Jewish Lights, 2009).

And Jacob drew close to his father Isaac; and he felt him, and said: "The voice is the voice of Jacob, but the hands are the hands of Esau." And he did not recognize him, because his hands were hairy like those of his brother Esau; so he blessed him.

Genesis 27:22–23

Doubting, Yet Doing Anyway

Wondering, doubting, not being sure, and yet blessing anyway. These verses from the intriguing familial story, starring two of our patriarchs, and which contain so many elements—trickery, deceit, favoritism, doubt, complicity, disappointment, competition, betrayal, and blessing, to name just a few—have particular resonance for me.

They highlight the very messiness, untidiness, and seeming arbitrariness of life. And yet, ultimately, they result in a blessing anyway. Just as in Genesis, where we read that God creates the earth and all that fills it out of *tohu va'vohu* (astonishing emptiness and formlessness), so too in these verses, something good comes out of the chaos or formlessness of normal life.

These verses also allude to some of the ways in which we can know another person, and through which we allow ourselves to be known. "The voice is the voice of Jacob, yet the hands are the hands of Esau." Surely, it's no accident that voices and hands are the elements of our humanity that are the ones via which Isaac is confused. We make ourselves known best through our words and through our actions.

These verses speak to my experience of being a Jew, a child, a twin, a sibling, a parent, a spouse, and a rabbi.

Rabbi Karen Companez was ordained at Hebrew Union College–Jewish Institute of Religion in May 2002, and since then, she has served as the rabbi of Temple Beth El in Flint, Michigan. Prior to entering the rabbinate, Rabbi Companez was instrumental in the establishment of a lay-led Reform congregation in Melbourne, Australia, and she was one of the founding members of the (now worldwide) Reform Zionist youth movement, Netzer, in Melbourne. Rabbi Companez is committed to building Jewish community and to helping people feel that their contributions to the community are of value.

So the offering went on ahead of him; and he himself lodged that night in the camp. And he rose up that night, and took his two wives, and his two handmaids, and his eleven children, and passed over the ford of the Jabbok. And he took them, and sent them over the stream, and sent over that which he had. And Jacob was left alone; and there wrestled a man with him until the breaking of the day. And when he saw that he did not prevail against him, he touched the hollow of his thigh; and the hollow of Jacob's thigh was strained, as he wrestled with him. And he said: "Let me go, for the day breaks." And he said: "I will not let you go unless you bless me." And he said to him: "What is your name?" And he said: "Jacob." And he said: "Your name will no more be called Jacob, but Israel; for you have struggled with God and with men, and have prevailed." And Jacob asked him, and said: "Tell me, please, your name." And he said: "Wherefore is it that you ask for my name?" And he blessed him there. And Jacob called the name of the place Peniel: "For I have seen God face to face, and my life is preserved."

Genesis 32:22–31

Unless You Bless Me

I grew up in a Lutheran home and attended a Lutheran camp, a Lutheran college, and a Lutheran seminary. I was fairly bright and had a modicum of talent. I figured I'd go far in a career in the church and maybe help some folks along the way in the bargain. Who knew? Maybe I'd be an Assistant to a Bishop by the time I was in my 30s. Only . . .

Only I was gay. And being gay and in the church, let alone gay clergy, was outside the box in the mid-'70s. Way outside the box. I struggled with both my call to ministry and my call to be who I really was and love whomever I was created to love.

I left full-time parish ministry for many years always managing to hover at the edges helping out and preaching here and there. I wrestled with God and my sense that God was continuing to call me to serve in a fuller way—and along the road found many straight friends and allies in the church who were engaged in that struggle, as well.

During these years, it was this story of Jacob's wrestling with God and his determination to receive the blessing that also gave him a new name that was a still, small, steady voice in my life. "I will not let you go, unless you bless me."

Bless me? Yes, indeed, God is extravagantly generous. I grew up and so did the Evangelical Lutheran Church. I know this to be so; I served as pastor of Christ the Shepherd Lutheran Church in Altadena, California for nine years. Six years ago my partner and I were joined in Holy Union there. And, I guess I have a new name, though "Honey" is maybe not so dignified as "Israel."

Father John M. Kauffman, age fifty-eight, is married to Professor Emeritus Thomas R. Wortham, UCLA. They live in semi-retirement in rural Ohio on Buckeye Lake. Father Kauffman is now serving as Assistant to the Rector at St. Luke's Episcopal Church, in nearby Granville.

Wrestling with God

The saga of the patriarch Jacob has always been particularly meaningful for me. Not that I have been quite the scoundrel that Jacob could be, but I, too, have done a lot of wrestling with God in my life. For me, faith has always been a struggle.

Jacob means "supplanter," but I've always thought of him as "Jacob the chiseler." He robbed his brother, Esau, deceived his blind and aged father, Isaac, then fled to the old family homestead in Haran and his wily uncle Laban, in whom Jacob met his match.

You know the story of their mutual conniving. Twenty years of indentured servitude for his two wives and flocks; then creeping off in the night.

As Jacob journeys back home, he is fearful about confronting his brother Esau, who vowed to destroy him. Reaching the Jabbok, a Jordan tributary, during the night Jacob sends his family and possessions across, and he is left alone in the moonlight.

Now comes the strange account of a mysterious being who struggles with Jacob all night long. As dawn is breaking, the stranger touches Jacob's thigh, wrenching it from its socket. Gradually Jacob realizes with whom he is wrestling. When the mysterious figure says to the crippled Jacob, "Let me go for the day is breaking," Jacob gasps, "I will not let you go unless you bless me."

When asked his name, he replies, "Jacob." And the mysterious stranger responds, "Your name will no longer be Jacob"—the chiseler—"but Israel"—contender with God—"for you have struggled with God and with men and have prevailed." Now, with a ready heart, the struggler with God limps off to his rendezvous with destiny.

I believe that Jacob's wrestling with God is symbolic of his inner struggle. With his checkered past and his impending confrontation with Esau, now he is at peace, because he has the assurance of divine acceptance.

Earlier in my own life, I had prolonged periods of depression, accompanied with vague but powerful feelings of guilt, of

not "measuring up," and God would seem far away. I understand something of Jacob's "wrestling," and "limping on his
thigh." I find comfort that Jacob's enemy becomes a friend,
whom he will not release without his gracious blessing. This
thought is captured in the New Testament book of I John, "If
our heart condemns us, God is greater than our heart." And
that is my peace in the struggle.

Thomas W. Strieter is a retired Lutheran minister and professor of
theology and ethics. His ministry has been divided between parish and
academia. He and his wife, Doris, have a long history of activism in
civil rights, peace movements, and other human rights and social justice issues.

Wrestling

Some say Jacob wrestled an angel—some say it was God. But,
importantly, one of the primary formative encounters between
Jacob and the divine was not worship, not just an act of obedience, but wrestling. Striving, and persistently struggling until one
receives a blessing.

One of my housemates plays capoeira, and I love to watch
his group play. It looks like dancing, and there's rhythm and
flowing movement. But it's also assuredly fighting, and people
get hit and knocked over. I trust something implicitly about this
style, developed by enslaved Afro-Brazilian people, because it
blurs the line between dance and fight.

Jacob has a night of intense struggle, of fierce intimacy with
God, and walks away with a blessing, but limping. Or, he walks
away with a limp, but with a blessing.

I grew up in the United Methodist Church, and I was ordained in an American Baptist/Alliance of Baptists congregation. I'm in touch with a couple hundred congregations every year in my current work with an interfaith non-profit. I preach regularly across the spectrum of mainline Protestantism. I love the local church with a passion matched by few other commitments. But of course, (those who also love the local church will understand the 'of course' here) I also hate it. When congregations embody their call to be the body of Jesus in the world, when they work and pray for justice, when they create spaces of radical welcome for those who are not often welcomed—I love them. But sometimes they don't do that. Sometimes they seem to miss that particular call and instead respond to a call for adequacy, a call for the status quo, some other call that I don't think Jesus is actually issuing. I have seen the power of congregations embodying their calls. And I hate it when they don't try to do so.

Some, in the face of such disappointment, are called away from the local congregation. Some are called to other denominations or faith traditions. Some are called to other venues: to stop bothering to show up in worship and instead spend their fighting and dancing energy in other ways.

But the local congregation is my vocation. And I expect to fight with them, and dance with them, all the years of my life. And I expect to walk away with a blessing, but limping. Or, to walk away with a limp, but with a blessing.

Reverend David Weasley has served as the Community and Congregational Relations Coordinator at The Night Ministry since September of 2010. He is an ordained American Baptist pastor, and serves on the board of the Association of Welcoming and Baptists, the national Baptist LGBTQ organization. He lives with his partner and about a dozen others in a co-op in Chicago. He is a graduate of Oberlin College and the Chicago Theological Seminary.

These are the generations of Jacob. Joseph, being seven-
teen years old, was feeding the flock with his brothers,
being still a youth even with the sons of Bilhah, and with
the sons of Zilpah, his father's wives; and Joseph brought
bad reports of them to their father. Now Israel loved
Joseph more than all his children, because he was the son
of his old age; and he made him a coat of many colors.
And when his brothers saw that their father loved him
more than all his brothers, they hated him, and could not
speak peaceably to him. . . .

Genesis: 37:2–4

. . . And Joseph said to his brothers, and to his father's
household: "I will go up, and I will tell Pharaoh, and will
say to him, 'My brothers, and my father's household, who
were in the land of Canaan, have come to me; and the men
are shepherds, for they have been keepers of cattle; and
they have brought their flocks, and their herds, and all that
they have.' And it shall come to pass, when Pharaoh calls
to you, and will say, 'What is your occupation?' That you
will say: 'Your servants have been keepers of cattle from
our youth even until now, both we, and our fathers;' that
you may dwell in the land of Goshen; for every shepherd is
an abomination to the Egyptians."

Genesis 46:31–34

The Story of Joseph
Genesis 37:2–46:34

The story of Joseph and his "coat of many colors" has been a
favorite of mine since childhood. As a child I found refuge in
the story for Joseph did not fit in. He was doted upon by his

father and despised by his brothers. Joseph was a dreamer and loved to tell of his dreams which only made his brothers more jealous.

As a young boy I too was a dreamer. I was picked on by the other kids and just did not fit in. No matter how my parents tried to help, I remained an outcast. I would escape into books and/or worlds of my own imagination. One of those books was the story of Joseph and his coat of many colors (children's Bible version).

The book taught me that it was okay to dream, to hope and to pray. Often my childhood world involved talking to God. I dreamed of becoming a Catholic priest. I did eventually go to seminary to study to be a priest. However, while at seminary, I discovered my sexuality, and I was called first and foremost to come out and be who I was. This was not compatible with the Catholic Church and so I had to leave.

Like Joseph I found myself in odd situations, traveled to strange towns such as Worcester, Dorchester, San Francisco, and Palm Springs. Throughout my wanderings the story of Joseph stayed with me. The original cantata written by Andrew Lloyd Webber and lyrics by Tim Rice originally came to my attention in high school. I ended up with every version ever recorded and the message of the dreamer who stayed faithful remained with me.

In Palm Springs I was forty-two when I found myself listening to the old dream to be a minister. I thought I was crazy. I was living on disability. I had a nice home and was making ends meet. However, much like the dreamer, I had to listen to the prophetic voice that compelled me. I applied for seminary and ended up being accepted.

In the end, much like Joseph, I serve the Great King, the King of Heaven. I am a minister serving at a congregation in the San Fernando Valley in Los Angeles. I have two master's degrees and am starting work on my doctorate. All this was made possible just as in the story of Joseph, through trust and perseverance and holding on to my dreams.

Reverend Joseph Shore-Goss is the Pastor of Congregational Care and Spiritual Life at Metropolitan Community Church in the Valley, located in North Hollywood, California. He is a graduate of Claremont School of Theology from which he holds both a Master of Divinity and a Master of Arts with a concentration in Pastoral Care. He is legally married to Rev. Dr. Robert E. Shore-Goss.

And Israel said to Joseph: "Do not your brothers tend the flock in Shechem? Come, and I will send you to them." And he said to him: "Here I am." And he said to him: "Go please now, see whether it is well with your brothers, and well with the flock; and bring me back word." And he sent him out of the vale of Hebron, and he came to Shechem. And a certain man found him, and, behold, he was wandering in the field. And the man asked him, saying: "What are you seeking?" And he said: "I seek my brothers. Tell me, please, where they are tending the flock." And the man said: "They have departed from here; for I heard them say, 'Let us go to Dothan.'" And Joseph went after his brothers, and found them in Dothan.

Genesis 37:13–17

Who's That Man?

In this small interlude, Jacob sends his son Joseph out to meet his brothers who are tending flocks in a distant field. Maybe Joseph had reached the age of maturity, or maybe Jacob had simply had enough of the dreams and the coat. Joseph gets lost. Along comes a man who asks Joseph what he is looking for. When Joseph tells him, he answers, to use a relatively contemporary idiom, "They went that-a-way."

We don't know his name and we don't know how he knew. He showed a simple courtesy, and by doing so he set in motion a succession of events that resulted in the central story of Judaism, the inheritors of the biblical tradition, including Christianity and Islam, and the world we know today. Without him, there would have been no Moses, no Jesus, no Mohammed, no you, and no me.

These few verses lead me to conclude that there is no such thing as an incidental action. Everything counts. To maintain a consciousness of the potential of even the smallest action is to live in holiness. If I can succeed in remembering that, and perhaps persuading a few others, we may be able to avoid disastrous words and deeds and, instead, bring redemption.

Jack Moline has been rabbi of Agudas Achim Congregation in Alexandria, Virginia since 1987. He also serves as Director of Public Policy for the Rabbinical Assembly. Most importantly, he is husband of Ann and father of three almost perfect adult children.

Anonymous Power:
The Stranger in the Field

Background: Jacob asked Joseph to check on his brothers who were tending their flock near Shechem. Joseph answered the request with one word, *Heneini*, "Here I am." Elsewhere in the Bible, that answer suggests a daunting test. Here too there is danger for Joseph. Shechem is the place where his brothers had slaughtered locals in retribution for their sister's rape (seduction? love?). Once Joseph reaches Shechem, he wanders until a stranger in the field addresses him, "What are you seeking?" Joseph explains that he is looking for his shepherd brothers. The stranger replies that they have already left, but that he has overheard them say that they were headed to Dothan. Joseph proceeds to Dothan and finds his brothers. A series of events unfolds: Joseph's brothers sell Joseph into slavery. Joseph later achieves great power and uses it to help others. The stranger in the field pivots Joseph toward fulfillment of his destiny.

A role model: "What are you seeking?" The stranger's question is often our own, whether we are lost and seeking a way forward or are in search of reconnecting with loved ones. As a stranger in the field, we may surprise ourselves by possessing valuable information. We may also never know the significance to another of a simple word, a reaching out, or the offering of direction. The stranger in the field is a hero in the biblical tale because he is essential to the unfolding of Joseph's destiny. His anonymity only adds to the mystery of whether he is an angel or a man at the right place at the right time or both. As a hero his action instructs us that when we act selflessly, we too are angel-like. The stranger in the field reminds us that we cannot anticipate the enormous impact that we may make on another in the unfolding mystery of life.

Rabbi Elie Kaplan Spitz has served as the spiritual leader of Congregation B'nai Israel (Tustin, California) since 1988. He has authored two books for Jewish Lights Publishing: *Does the Soul Survive?: A Jewish Journey to Belief in Afterlife, Past Lives, and Living with Purpose* (2000) and *Healing from Despair: Choosing Wholeness in a Broken World* (2008).

And he blessed them that day, saying: "By you shall Israel bless, saying, 'May God make you as Ephraim and as Manasseh;'" and he set Ephraim before Manasseh.

Genesis 48:20

The Blessing of Ephraim and Manasseh

Every Friday evening, as people gather around their Sabbath dinner tables, parents rise up to bless their children. After a busy week, often fraught with anxiety, stress and the emotionally-charged exchanges that typify the relationship between most parents and children, this moment of blessing is especially poignant and particularly optimistic. For a brief time, children are reminded of their parents' love for them. And parents are reminded of the promise that children hold for the entire world. These are moments filled with profound love and optimism. And in the midst of an unfolding Shabbat, we are truly given a glimpse of the world-to-come and the possibilities it holds for all of us.

These words, "May you be like Ephraim and Manasseh," followed by the familiar three-fold priestly blessing, "May God bless you and keep you. . . ." are among the most loving that a parent can offer. While the words are shaped entirely by Jewish tradition, they are formed in the hearts of parents as they ask for Divine blessing for their children, inviting God to help their children fulfill their dreams even as the protective and nurturing Divine spirit hovers over them.

Jewish tradition invites us to speak these words of blessing specifically through the legacy of Ephraim and Manasseh, children of the biblical Joseph, children whom grandfather Jacob took as his own. In this selfless deed, which is based on Genesis 48:3–20, Jacob acts to continue the line of the biblical patriarchs (and we would add: matriarchs) through his grandchildren, born to him by his son Joseph, and his *Egyptian* wife Asnat. The Bible is not concerned with her particular family of origin for she, like so many like her who live in our midst in today's community, chose to cast her lot with the Jewish people, voluntarily establish a Jewish home and raise Jewish children. Joseph's family did not distance her or withhold their love for her or their children because of her non-Jewish origins. Would that we were able to do the same for those who have married into Judaism and joined the ranks of our families and communities. For her act of love, we have rewarded her with blessing—and included our children—but it is really she who has blessed us.

Rabbi Kerry M. Olitzky is the Executive Director of the Jewish Outreach Institute, the only national independent organization dedicated to bringing Judaism to interfaith families and the unaffiliated. A leader in the development of innovative Jewish education, particularly for adults, he has shaped training programs for clergy of all faiths, especially in the area of pastoral care and counseling in the Jewish community. He has done pioneering work in the area of Jewish Twelve Step spirituality, as well as Jewish Gerontology. He is a contributing editor for *Shma: A Journal of Jewish Responsibility* and is also the author of over seventy books and hundreds of articles in a variety of fields. His opinion pieces are published in leading publications throughout North America and in Israel.

*"And as for you, you meant evil against me; but God
meant it for good, to bring to pass, as it is this day, to keep
many people alive."*

Genesis 50:20

Redemption

One of the anchoring scriptures of my life has been Joseph's
response to his brothers at the end of Genesis: "You plotted
evil against me, but God turned it into good. . . ." (Genesis
50:20).

One cannot spend one's life ministering within a religious
institution without having the experience of being hurt and be-
trayed by the very people one is expected to see as "brothers
and sisters." Over and over again in situations where those in
positions of power have rejected my gifts and denigrated my
work, where self-destructive parishioners have tried to destroy
the good that was coming to fruition within the life of the
community, where mean-spirited individuals have stood in the
way of possibilities and potentialities, and where those within
the church who cared more about the bottom line than creating
shalom have momentarily seemed to triumph, I have held on to
this passage and waited for the day when what others meant for
evil, God would work for good.

I love that this story is so truthful. I love that it neither de-
nies the evil that can exist within our community nor gives way
to despondency or hopelessness in the face of that evil. I love
that this short passage takes one of the deep tragedies of scripture—a young man being nearly killed and then sold into slavery
by his own brothers—and makes of it a story of redemption.
This story offers me a God I can believe in . . . a God who

remains present and active even in the midst of life's gravest injustices and deepest sufferings.

The Very Reverend Sylvia Sweeney, Ph.D., is Dean and President of Bloy House/Episcopal Theological School at Claremont.

EXODUS

And the king of Egypt spoke to the Hebrew midwives, of whom the name of the one was Shiphrah, and the name of the other Puah; and he said: "When you do the office of a midwife to the Hebrew women, you are to look upon the birthstool: if it is a son, then you are to kill him; but if it is a daughter, then she is to live." But the midwives feared God, and did not do as the king of Egypt commanded them, but instead saved the male children alive. And the king of Egypt called for the midwives, and said to them: "Why have you done this thing, and saved the male children alive?" And the midwives said to Pharaoh: "Because the Hebrew women are not like the Egyptian women; for they are lively, and are delivered before the midwife comes to them." And God dealt well with the midwives; and the people multiplied, and became very mighty. And it came to pass, because the midwives feared God, that God made them houses. And Pharaoh charged all his people, saying: "Every son that is born you are to cast into the river, and every daughter you are to save alive."

Exodus 1:15–22

Children First

The example of the Hebrew midwives is clear. Because they fear God, and not Pharaoh, they demonstrate an extraordinary commitment to the well-being of their community. These women put children first, even at the risk of their own lives.

There are those who say that children are the future. I disagree. I believe children are to be welcomed as full members of the community right now. What would need to change in order for us to welcome children, as Shiphrah and Puah did?

At our church we have made changes to signal a shift in priorities. Worship is no longer an adult haven. Rather, we are making room for children to be present and to participate. There's a spot in the back of our worship space for toddlers and a small table for school-aged children to sit and work on crafts or coloring during worship. The teens sit resolutely along their own back row of chairs, unless it is their turn to lead worship, read Scripture, or play in our band. Children as young as three years old participate with their parents in leading the service. During our children's moment, the children bring a message to us that they prepare during Sunday School.

People ask me about the noise children can make. I reply that when children are interested and engaged, they are not disruptive. If an infant is fussy or a toddler really needs to move around, parents simply take them to the enclosed garden area just outside.

Our worship is enlivened by the presence of these young ones, and believe me, they have taken ownership of the church as full members, right now. To have the joy of nurturing these young ones, and to learn from them, is an extraordinary privilege.

We've heard of Moses. But what about the many other children Shiphrah and Puah saved? Those children grew up and participated in a movement for freedom, all because two women put children first. I am inspired by Shiphrah and Puah to welcome children and to look for ways to empower them to make a difference in their communities.

Reverend Sandie Richards, a California native, felt a call to urban ministry as a young adult. She attended seminary at Union Theological Seminary in New York City and was ordained in 1993 as a United Methodist minister. Rev. Richards currently serves as the pastor of First United Methodist Church of Los Angeles. She lives in Los Angeles with her husband Bill and their eleven year old son Woody.

And she opened it, and saw it, the child; and behold a boy that wept. And she had compassion on him, and said: "This is one of the Hebrews' children."

Exodus 2:6

Seeing Humanity in the Other

In the opening chapters of the Book of Exodus we read of Pharaoh's fear and mistrust of the Israelites. He is convinced that in the advent of war the Israelite men will fight on the side of Egypt's enemies. Pharaoh is so worried that he commands the midwives to kill all male Hebrew babies. When the midwives foil Pharaoh's plan he expands his quest for genocide: "Then Pharaoh charged all his people saying every boy that is born you shall throw into the Nile" (Exodus 1:22).

We can only assume that all the Egyptians, out of fear or conviction, followed Pharaoh's decree. When Moses is born his mother tries to save him by placing him in a basket (actually an ark) in the Nile. His sister, Miriam, stands by, waiting to see what will become of her brother. As she stands on the shore, she sees Pharaoh's daughter's servants find the basket and give it to their mistress. As she slowly pulls the blanket away from the baby's face, Miriam (and the reader) wonders what she will do. After all, she is the daughter of Pharaoh. She is charged, just like all of Egypt, to kill Israelite babies. Will she command her servants to throw the baby back into the Nile?

The Torah describes the scene: "When she opened it she saw it was a child, a boy crying. She took pity on him and said, 'This must be a Hebrew child.'" She makes this baby, whom she names Moses, her son.

And so I wonder what is it about this woman that makes her able to see the humanity of this child. Why doesn't she see what

her father sees, a dangerous enemy? Why does she see an inno-
cent babe? We are taught in the Torah that every human being is
created in the image of God. Nevertheless, when we look at
people, what is it that we see? Can we see the humanity in
someone who looks differently than we do? Can we see the
humanity of someone across a political divide? Can we see the
humanity of a Palestinian child, or just a potential enemy? I
think about this challenge a great deal and when I do, I remember the courage and strength of Pharaoh's daughter.

Rabbi Debra Newman Kamin has been the spiritual leader of Am
Yisrael Congregation in Northfield, Illinois since 1990. Am Yisrael is
one of the largest Conservative congregations to be headed by a
woman rabbi. Rabbi Newman Kamin serves as Secretary of the
International Rabbinical Assembly. She also serves on the Chancellor's
Cabinet of the Jewish Theological Seminary of America. Married and
the mother of three children, she and her family reside in Highland
Park, Illinois.

And Moses said to God: "Behold, when I come to the children of Israel, and shall say to them, 'The God of your ancestors has sent me to you' and they shall say to me, 'What is God's name?', What shall I say to them?" And God said to Moses: "I AM THAT I AM," and God said: "Thus shall you say to the children of Israel: I AM has sent me to you." And God said moreover to Moses: "Thus shall you say to the children of Israel: the Eternal One, the God of your ancestors, the God of Abraham, the God of Isaac, and the God of Jacob, has sent me to you; this is My name forever, and this is My memorial for all generations. . . ."

Exodus 3:13–15

Getting to Know You

During our orientation to the seminary, a psychologist led us through the following exercise: We sat in circles of about eight seminarians. One would start and ask the person on his right, "Who are you?" That person would answer then ask the person on his right. This continued for about a dozen rounds of the circle, and each time the person answering was to add something more revealing.

At the end, the psychologist, who was going from circle to circle listening to a sampling of answers, remarked that he had not heard anyone share anything that was particularly personal or intimate. For a while I felt guilty that I had not been more forthcoming with my classmates.

Then I happened to read Exodus 3, and a light went on! If people really want to know who I am, they will not just sit in a circle and ask me. They will stick around and find out who I am, spending time with me, observing me, interacting with me in all

kinds of different situations, sharing small talk and eventually
more personal and intimate revelations. This is how genuine
friendships are fostered.

I believe this is why God gives such a mysterious answer to
Moses when Moses asks who he is. "I am who I am" is not simply a reference to God's infinity and ultimate otherness, but is
an invitation to spend time with him, to interact with him in all
kinds of circumstances, whether challenging or comforting. This
was the beginning of God's self-revelation in mighty deeds and
of the daily interaction between God and the people of Israel.

This lesson is very important in our culture of instant grati-
fication. If we want strong and lasting relationships, we need to
give them time, respect their mystery, and dedicate ourselves to
each other in good times and bad. It is in this kind of patient
dedication and respect for others that true love can grow and
true peace be nurtured.

The Most Reverend Larry Silva has been the Roman Catholic
Bishop of Honolulu, which includes all the Hawaiian Islands, since
July 2005. Born in Honolulu in 1949, he was raised in the Oakland
area and served as a priest in the Diocese of Oakland for thirty years.
His seminary training was at St. Patrick's Seminary in Menlo Park,
California.

Encountering the "I Am"

One of the most spiritually paradigmatic scriptures for my faith
as a Christian is Moses' initial encounter with the living God in
Exodus 3:13–15. This passage has been a source of spiritual
insight in my childhood, during the challenges of adolescence,

and in the throes of mid-life. As a child, I was shaped by the cultural nuances of a northern New Jersey upbringing, especially in regard to religion. I enjoyed a distinct religious affinity with my Jewish friends by virtue of our shared Judeo-Christian heritage. Despite our differences, we all claimed the story of the Exodus as foundational to our faiths. I recall as a child watching Cecil B. DeMille's *The Ten Commandments* as an annual broadcast event on television in the 1970s during the Passover and Easter seasons. The impressive portrayal of the Red Sea's parting never failed to captivate me. Yet, it was Moses' enigmatic encounter with God who identifies Himself as "I AM WHO I AM" at the burning bush that particularly intrigued my heart. What an astonishing and terrifying experience! "Glad it was Moses and not me," I would innocently think with a sense of childish relief. Yet, I was profoundly naïve about the biblical depth of that event and the God whose dramatic appearance to Moses would be a turning point for him, the nation of Israel, and eventually myself.

My own personal encounter with the LORD came at age seventeen in an unexpected way. I was transformed by the awakening of my soul as I made a personal profession of faith in Jesus Christ as my Savior. Now I was confronted with the "I Am" through the eyes of a redeeming faith. Jesus' numerous references to "I Am" in the Gospels afforded me an even deeper understanding of how God intimately invites me into His presence. My personal encounter with God prompted me to embrace the miracle of the burning bush as analogous to my own life. In the words of John Wesley, "I felt my heart strangely warmed" and now began to discern by faith what had drawn the child by sight. Still, in abject humility I could not even begin to contain the vast implications of God's self-disclosure at the "I Am." All I could do as I beheld the "I Am" was bow before Him in complete surrender and marvel at His amazing grace!

Now at the crossroads of mid-life, I find myself at that transitional stage of my life where I am predictably closer to entering the fullness of eternity. As I reflect and reassess the totality of my days thus far, I yearn for the merciful care of the "I Am" as my Shepherd who meets my every need (Psalm 23:1). The diminishing of my mortal capacities with age summons me to rest in my relationship with the LORD who is from "everlasting to everlasting" (Psalm 90:2). Even as my life changes and ebbs, the uncreated "I Am" remains the same, "yesterday, today, and forever" (Hebrews 13:8). Amidst the anxieties and uncertainties which plague my earthly sojourn, in Him I find both a consolation for my soul and an unfailing anchor for my faith. Amen.

Reverend George J. Mendes is an ordained Southern Baptist minister presently serving on active duty as a U.S. Navy chaplain. He earned his B.A. from the Moody Bible Institute in Chicago, his Master of Divinity degree from Southwestern Baptist Theological Seminary in Fort Worth, Texas, and his Doctor of Ministry degree from Fuller Theological Seminary in Pasadena, California. He is married and has three children.

I Will Be What I Will Be
Exodus 3:14

The most mystical, magical moment in the Torah for me occurs when Moses encounters God in the desert in the form of the burning bush. Moses asks God's name, and God replies with the perplexing response: "*Ehyeh asher ehyeh*," best translated as "I will be what I will be."

The hubris of choosing the virtually untranslatable, indefinable name of God as the Torah text that speaks to me most is not lost on me. When Moses speaks to God at the burning bush, their encounter is so deeply personal, so indicative of Moses' greater search for meaning and purpose that it feels almost voyeuristic to lay claim to such a phrase as being my "favorite."

Yet my love for this text did not actually come from reading it in the Torah. When my husband and I were rabbinical students, he gave me a book about the first woman rabbi, Fraulein Rabbiner Regina Jonas. Regina Jonas perished in Auschwitz in 1944, and her story was virtually unknown until a collection of her personal documents was discovered after the collapse of the Berlin Wall. Among these documents was a photo of Regina Jonas taken shortly after her ordination. She looks serious, compassionate, and strong. On the back of the photo, along with the date, she had inscribed a text from the Torah: *Ehyeh asher ehyeh.* I will be what I will be.

Years later, I still get goose bumps when I imagine her writing those words. They sound both defiant and unsure, as if she is daring others to doubt her while still wrestling with a calling that seemed to defy her own beloved tradition. In using God's own words, she not only shows herself as truly being *b'tzelem Elohim*, made in God's image, but also seems to give us a new understanding of what God might have meant with that strange response. There is an acceptance and a challenge in those words. We can be no more than what we are meant to be, yet what we are meant to be is limitless and beyond our wildest imagination.

Rabbi Amy Feder is the Rabbi at Congregation Temple Israel in St. Louis, where she works alongside her husband, Rabbi Michael Alper. A St. Louis native, she attended the University of Michigan and Hebrew Union College. She and Rabbi Alper are the proud parents of one son, Jonah.

*And Moses said to the Eternal One: "Oh my Eternal One,
I am not a man of words, neither yesterday, nor before that
day, nor since You have spoken to Your servant; for I am
slow of speech, and of a slow tongue." And the Eternal
One said to him: "Who has made man's mouth? Or who
makes a man dumb, or deaf, or seeing, or blind? Is it not I
the Eternal One? Now therefore go, and I will be with your
mouth, and teach you what you will speak."*

Exodus 4:10–12

Not Good Enough . . . But Still Called

When I was in sixth grade I had to give a speech in front of my
whole school—students, teachers, administrators and parents. It
was a graduation ceremony from elementary school and my
teacher had gotten me to give a speech based on a paper I had
written earlier in the year. The trouble was, she made me memo-
rize it. I got a minute or two into the speech and forgot the next
lines. I was devastated. An eternity seemed to pass as I sat there
silent before the crowd, totally lost. My teacher finally remembered a line or two from my paper, and I took hold of that and
was able to finish. Unfortunately, the line that she gave me was
well past where I had stopped. So there was a lot that got
skipped. This embarrassment stuck with me. From that point
on, I was always worried about speaking in public. I shied away
from it every time I could. When God called me to be a pastor,
I protested immediately: "But I'm not very good with words! I
can't do public speaking. I don't want to do public speaking!"
God reminded me of Moses, and what he told Moses after he
complained. God then told me to "Go, and I will be with you as
you speak, and I will instruct you in what to say." While I still
wished for an Aaron, I moved ahead as a pastor and preacher,

trusting that God would always help. So far, I think we've done pretty well.

Over the years, I've learned, like Moses, that none of us are good enough, or well-spoken enough, or smart enough, or talented enough, or holy enough to represent God to the world . . . yet he chooses us anyway. In our inadequacy, we quickly learn to depend on God. In his gracious, marvelous way, he gives us everything we need, and sometimes even more! If you're feeling "not good enough," remember Moses, and trust that God loves you and knows exactly what he's doing. If God is calling you, he will provide.

Reverend David Deans has been a pastor for eight years. He was on his way to veterinary school when God first called him into the ministry. Reverend Deans has served churches near Annapolis and Baltimore. He is now the Associate Pastor of Oakdale Emory United Methodist Church in Olney, Maryland, where he lives with his wife, Deb, and their two kids.

And afterwards Moses and Aaron came, and said to Pharaoh: "Thus says the Eternal One, the God of Israel, 'Let My people go, that they may celebrate a festival for Me in the wilderness.'" And Pharaoh said: "Who is the Eternal One, that I should heed His voice to let Israel go? I do not know the Eternal One, and moreover I will not let Israel go." And they said: "The God of the Hebrews has met with us. Let us go, we pray you, three days' journey into the wilderness, and sacrifice to the Eternal One our God lest God strike us with pestilence, or with the sword." And the king of Egypt said to them: "Why do you, Moses and Aaron, disturb the people from their work? Get to your labors."

Exodus 5:1–4

Who Am I That I Should Go to Pharaoh?

There is a banner that hangs outside of my church that reads, "God Is Still Speaking." My denomination, the United Church of Christ (UCC), loves this phrase that echoes the rich Jewish tradition of the Oral Torah. We appreciate the fact that to apply the ageless wisdom of Scripture to today's complex, multi-faceted challenges demands an ongoing and open-minded encounter with the Word of God. Thus I can find myself sometimes debating with Christian fundamentalists who base their belief in Creationism and their opposition to gay rights on a literal understanding of a collection of passages from Genesis and Leviticus. As a result, as a progressive Christian clergyman, I have to look to verses of the Torah that can sing to my heart without the "baggage" of my debates with fundamentalists. Fortunately, I do not have to look too far for compelling passages that speak to my heart and inspire me to action.

Much of the Book of Exodus recounts the showdown between Moses and the Pharaoh. The repeated confrontation of people of compassion and faith with the intractable arrogance of temporal power actually comforts me. It strengthens my personal resolve not to let my own level of frustration overtake me any more than Moses did.

Moses' escalating confrontation with an evermore intractable Pharaoh reminds me that today's progressives are part of a very long and continuing tradition. I came of age during the era of Civil Rights and Vietnam. I have seen the intentional blindness, selfishness, and the towering arrogance of some occupants of the Oval Office. My values, my life view, and my understanding of politics and social change were shaped by witnessing courageous believers in peace and civil rights criticized, rebuffed, refuted, and ignored by the leaders who had the power and ability to bring about change and to foster justice. Even the Pharaoh's allegations (Exodus 5:8), "They are a lazy people . . ." is an eerie precursor for Ronald Reagan's classic—and totally specious—story of "welfare queens driving welfare Cadillacs."

So the timeless wisdom of Exodus still gives me heart when today's powerful temporal leaders refuse to listen to my voice and the voice of others calling out for the end of oppression in so many areas. There is, indeed, nothing new under the sun. I can turn to the stories in Exodus and, like the old spiritual says, "Take my stand where Moses stood."

Reverend Douglas Stivison is an ordained minister in the United Church of Christ and is the pastor of First Congregational United Church of Christ in Haworth, New Jersey. He is the former editor of *The Living Pulpit* magazine and a former vice-president of the *Wall Street Journal*.

And God spoke to Moses and said to him, "I am the Eternal One [YHWH]. And I appeared to Abraham, to Isaac, and to Jacob as El Shaddai, but by My name YHWH I did not make Myself known to them."

Exodus 6:2–3

Interbreathing

The verses are from Exodus, chapter 3:14–15, and chapter 6:2–3, when God (at the Burning Bush and later in Egypt) says to Moses that the name by which God was known to the patriarchs and matriarchs is no longer the name that will free the people from slavery. Instead there must be a new name for God—"YHWH."

What does this mean to me? That in a time of profound crisis, the name of God must change. And that today we must draw on the ancient name "YHWH" not to mask it by saying "Adonai, Lord," but to pronounce it with no vowels—not "Yahweh" or "Jehovah" but "YyyyHhhhWwwwHhhh," a breath. The interbreathing of all life. Not a word in Hebrew, or Sanskrit, or Latin, or Greek, or English—but a breath in all of them. And not only human breath—for all life upon this planet breathes. What we breathe in is what the trees breathe out; what we breathe out is what the trees breathe in. We breathe each other into life. And this very interbreathing of oxygen and CO_2 is now in crisis—causing what we call the climate crisis. This crisis in the future of all life on Earth is a crisis in the "YHWH" name of God. So we need to say in our blessings not "Lord" and "*melech ha'olam*, King of the universe," but "Yahh" and "*ruach ha'olam*, Breath/Wind/Spirit of the world." We need to be aware that the Instruction, "Do not take My name in vain," means "Be fully aware that every breath you breathe is My Name, the Interbreathing you share with all of life."

Rabbi Arthur Waskow, director of The Shalom Center, www.theshalomcenter.org, is the author of many books on Jewish thought and practice and on public policy—most recently, a book co-authored with Rabbi Phyllis Berman, *Freedom Journeys: The Tale of Exodus and Wilderness Across Millennia* (Jewish Lights, 2011).

"... Our cattle will also go with us; there will not be a hoof left behind; for from it we must take to serve the Eternal One our God; and we will not know with what we are to serve the Eternal One, until we arrive there."

Exodus 10:26

Serving God

So much of our scriptural reading seems to put us into a very specific and precise spot. Do not veer to the right or to the left, do not add or subtract from it.

The sentence I chose means a lot to me because it says that things are not always equal and that we do not know the circumstances to which life will project us. I believe that when the time comes and the situation is ripe we will be reached by the Divine imperative that is specific to that time and place. It is for the same reason that the Bible tells us that there will be a place where God will choose to make His Presence dwell therein, but it did not give us the location until we got there; and then we only found out once we got there that it was Jerusalem.

This verse is so important to me that I've made it my message on the screen saver of my computer.

Rabbi Zalman Schachter-Shalomi, author of *Paradigm Shift*, *From Age-ing to Sage-ing*, *Wrapped in a Holy Flame*, and *Jewish With Feeling*, is professor emeritus at Temple University and past holder of the World Wisdom Chair at Naropa University. He is the founder of Aleph, Alliance for Jewish Renewal and is Spiritual Director of Yesod, Foundation for a Jewish Future.

*And the Eternal One spoke to Moses and Aaron in the
land of Egypt, saying: "This month will be to you the beginning of months; it will be the first month of the year for
you. . . ."*

*. . . And it came to pass on that very day that the Eternal
One did take the children of Israel out of the land of
Egypt by their hosts.*

Exodus 12

Exodus and Liberation

The events related to Passover in the Book of Exodus and the
Christian celebration of Lent and Easter are intrinsically inter-
related. For Christians including myself, Lent marks the forty
days leading up to Easter, the memorial of what we believe to
be Jesus' resurrection from the dead. While Lent's meaning is
most immediately derived from the gospel account of Jesus
having spent forty days fasting and praying alone in the desert,
where he successfully resisted Satan's temptations, the forty days
of Lent also have Old Testament roots. Most notable are the
forty days and nights Noah, his family, and a slew of animals
spent in an ark—according to the Book of Genesis—before
being safely delivered to begin life anew in a formerly sinful
world literally washed clean by God.

To me, these various scriptures speak strongly of liberation.
Passover and Lent annually bring to my mind humankind's past
and present deliverance from oppressive forces, whether they be
theological concepts like sin or the Devil or more historic,
power-mongering world leaders such as the pharaohs of ancient
Egypt or Hitler and his xenophobic Nazis. Today, I would count
some government officials among our oppressors, especially

when it comes to their continued refusal to recognize the human dignity of immigrants or to extend full equality as American citizens to members of the GLBT community.

Fortunately, both historical and scriptural records reveal that the oppressor is always struck down in the end. The more strongly the oppressors dig in their heels and refuse to grant freedom and equality to others, the more they seal their own doom. This seems especially true to me of Pharaoh in the Book of Exodus, who learned a lesson in divine liberation the hard way when he continuously denied freedom to Moses and the Hebrews. I see more recent evidence of this time-honored "fall of the mighty" in the wave of revolution that has swept so many Middle Eastern countries. This gives me great hope, both as a man of faith and as a human being.

The Most Reverend Christopher M. Carpenter is bishop of the Reformed Catholic Church Diocese of St. George, which covers the western United States. He also serves as a full-time hospice chaplain, a successful fundraiser and grant writer, and a published film, theater, and pop culture critic. Bishop Carpenter resides in Long Beach, California.

Leaving Egypt

Every Sunday, growing up, my family piled into the station wagon and drove the ten blocks through our affluent neighborhood to our church in the local village. We were such regulars that I had a perfect attendance record for eight years running; I know this, because I still have the attendance reward pins that I received at the end of each church school year to prove it! How did I spend so much time at church as a young child, in youth group, and at church camp every summer, without ever hearing the Exodus narrative? It wasn't until I lived in Central America in the mid-1980s, to learn Spanish and history, that I heard about and glimpsed, first-hand, the Exodus.

While attending a Spanish language school in San Jose, Costa Rica, I started attending a small church in a working-class housing development. On the edge of the neighborhood, hundreds of families had moved onto undeveloped land and built houses out of corrugated tin and cardboard, in hopes of creating a better life in the city for themselves and their children.

This pop-up settlement—and it was one of many that had sprung up, seemingly overnight, on the fringes of the city—had no infrastructure: no plumbing, no clean water, no electricity, no common outhouses even. The settlement was perched on a hillside that became treacherous during the rainy (muddy) season. Most of the settlement residents did not know how to read or write and had never navigated city life. Instead of attending school, children spent the days selling *chicle* gum on the streets, trekking through the mud to collect water from the single open faucet in the vicinity, or tending the small, open fires used for cooking.

My church, *Getsemani*, was committed to working with these new neighbors. Once introductions had been made and a burgeoning partnership formed, people from the church met with people from the settlement, to work on identifying priorities and learning about community organizing principles. On Sundays, we met for worship, and read and interpreted the biblical narratives in relation to daily life. Abstract interpretation was not acceptable. The question always came back to, "And what does this mean for you, for this community, for Costa Rica, for the world?" The Exodus narrative—and the many events within that narrative—was *the* central story for our discussions. The

Exodus narrative gave meaning and context to current experiences of moving from the country to the city; from one land to another; from poverty and overwhelming difficulties to hope; from being forgotten to being remembered, by both God and other people.

At the church I grew up in, I had learned that it was important to arrive at church on time, sit still during choir anthems, say the prayers, receive communion, and—above all—try to be nice to others. At the church in Costa Rica, where I really grew up, I began to learn about what it might mean to become a practitioner of the ways of Jesus. I was also told, in kindness, that to be a practitioner is extremely difficult for those of us who come from the Empire—the Land of Pharaoh, so to speak—and I have found that to be true.

The Reverend Jennifer Cleveland returned to California's Bay Area to finish up her M.Div. after living in Costa Rica for several years. She has been ordained as a priest in the Episcopal Church for over seventeen years, working in churches in Eastern Washington, Chicago, and Oregon. Currently, she serves as the Lower School Chaplain (PreK–5th grade) at Oregon Episcopal School in Portland. In addition to travel, she likes living in the Pacific Northwest, where, regularly, she has to make the decision of whether or not to spend the weekend in the mountains or at the coast.

*And the Eternal One said to Moses: "Why do you cry out
to Me? Tell the children of Israel to go forward. . . ."*

Exodus 14:15

The Risk of Faith, That First Step

My favorite Bible verse is Exodus 14:15. The Israelites had peti-
tioned Pharaoh over and over and afflicted him with plagues
until he finally let the enslaved Israelites go. While they were
going, however, Pharaoh changed his mind yet again and sent
his army out into the wilderness to hunt them down and slaugh-
ter them. In this verse the Israelites are up against a wall. They
are pinned against the sea and the whole Egyptian army is ar-
rayed against them. They are about to die. Moses cries out to
God and asks why God would bring them out and then have
them be killed. God says, "Watch as I will fight for you." Then
as the people are praying to God for help, verse 15 says: "Then
the LORD said to Moses, 'Why do you cry out to me? Tell the
Israelites to go forward.'" Another translation I like better as it
says, "Tell the people to quit praying and get going." That's
when God parts the sea and they are saved. It is fascinating to
note that the sea does not part until Moses takes the first step
into the waters. God does not do anything miraculous until a
step of faith is taken.

What a wonderful message and reminder that in our relationship with God we can pray, but at some point we need to
take a step in faith. Not until we take that step does God then
open the way. Too often we pray for the way to be opened and
wonder why it doesn't come. Taking that step of faith is essential.

As a recovering alcoholic, this passage has been especially
meaningful to me. When I was actively drinking twenty-five
years ago I knew there was something seriously wrong with my

life. I was trying everything I could think of to get my life on the right track, but no matter what I tried I could not manage to get my life in order. During those days I cried out to God often and wondered why he was not coming to my rescue. I wanted God to save me, fix my life. I wanted God to intervene and give me an instant and miraculous healing. Instead, God led me to Alcoholics Anonymous. I can't tell you how much I did not want to go there then, but now I can tell you it was the best thing I have ever done. God was trying to answer my prayers, but I was afraid to take the first step. Once I finally did, God opened up a whole new vista. God led me out of a life of slavery and bondage into a whole new life of freedom and joy.

Reverend Dr. Edward R. Treat grew up as an army brat in a large family of six boys and two girls. Once in recovery he returned to school and earned a B.A. at Western Washington State University. He earned an M.Div. and was ordained in the Evangelical Lutheran Church in America. Reverend Treat later completed his doctoral degree at Luther Seminary. He has previously served congregations in Nebraska and Minnesota and currently serves as Senior Pastor to a great congregation in Bloomington, Minnesota. He has a beautiful wife and four lovely children, thanks be to God.

Conversations with God and Man

Is there a limit to prayer? Exodus 14:15 offers a definitive answer: Yes. And the answer is placed in no less a personality than God who basically tells Moses to stop praying and start doing. With the Israelites caught between the Sea of Reeds and the Egyptian army, Moses had prayed for rescue long enough. Now was the time to encourage and motivate the Israelites to take fate into their own hands. And that's exactly what God instructs Moses to do.

Forget about the Israelites' predicament. How often do we fear the conversation that must take place, but which we simply cannot bring ourselves to initiate? There are all sorts of discussions that we ought to have with a supervisor, a spouse, a colleague or a friend, the results of which we fear. Our request for advancement might be denied, our revelation of an insult might be dismissed, our criticism of unwelcomed behaviors ignored, etc. We predict the outcomes without really knowing the future, and instead, spend hours sinking into our fears. We might as well pray to God endlessly, to no avail, for we are deaf to the divine voice saying, "Why do you cry out to Me?"

Another way one might translate Exodus 14:15 is as follows: "Then the Lord said to Moses, 'Why do you cry out to Me? Speak to the children of Israel, and they will go.'" In other words, don't fear the conversation. It's as if God is urging Moses to access his chutzpah. Not such bad advice! Is it sometimes an act of courage to initiate these conversations? Absolutely! And will those conversations effect some sort of brilliant resolution? Not necessarily, but one will never know until the conversation takes place.

Prayer holds a special place in my daily routine, and oddly enough, the God that I pray to is forever saying, "Why do you cry out to Me?" God moves me to speak to the people with whom I must really have the conversation, and I am forever amazed at how often those conversations end up being the answer to my prayers.

Rabbi Perry Raphael Rank is the spiritual leader of Midway Jewish Center in Syosset, Long Island. He is a former international president of the Rabbinical Assembly, the professional association of Conservative rabbis, and co-editor of *Moreh Derekh: The Rabbi's Manual of the Rabbinical Assembly.*

Then Moses and the children of Israel sang this song to
the Eternal One, and spoke, saying:
"I will sing to the Eternal One, for God is highly exalted;
The horse and his rider has God thrown into the sea;
The Eternal One is my strength and song;
And God is become my salvation;
This is my God, and I will glorify God;
My father's God, and I will exalt God. . . .

. . . The Eternal One shall reign for ever and ever."

Exodus 15:1–18

True Beauty

This is my God and I will glorify Him (*v'anveihu*); the God of my
father, and I will exalt Him (Exodus 15:2).

My bar mitzvah was pretty stressful. My *parashah* (Torah portion) was *B'shalach*, also known as *Shabbat Shirah* (Sabbath of
Song). I was the rabbi's eldest son, and somehow that meant
that I had the second longest *haftarah* of the year, *and* I also
chanted *Shirat Hayam* (Song by the Sea, Exodus 15). This re-
quired mastering a unique mode for chanting some of its verses.
However, despite my anxiety at facing over a thousand people,
this turned out to be a life-long gift. I have chanted *Shirat Hayam*
on *Shabbat Shirah* and on the seventh day of Passover for fifty
years, most meaningfully at my youngest daughter's bat mitzvah.
Its words are deep in my heart, and always with the soaring, joy-
ous lilt of that special melody. My chosen verse (Exodus 15:2)
stands out because it taught me two ways to serve God.

    Rabbi Ishmael says: Is it possible for flesh and blood to add
glory to the Creator? It simply means: I shall be beautiful before

Him in observing the commandments: I shall prepare for Him a beautiful *lulav* (palm branch used to celebrate the holiday of Sukkot), a beautiful *sukkah* (booth), beautiful *tzitzit* (fringes), and beautiful *t'fillin* (phylacteries). Abba Shaul says: Be like Him! Just as He is gracious and compassionate, so should you be gracious and compassionate (*Mekhilta Shirta* 3).

Rabbi Ishmael reads *v'anveihu* as "I will adorn Him." How could we mortals ever adorn the Creator, from whom all beauty comes? By performing ritual *mitzvot* (commandments) in the loveliest way, not with bare minimum compliance. God's *mitzvot* deserve enthusiasm and beauty. When I see a splendid *havdalah* set, or a radiant ark curtain, my inner voice chants this verse.

Abba Shaul reads *v'anveihu* as *ani v'hu*, I and He, be like God. We are partners. I cannot create worlds, but I can embody God's bountiful love, mercy, and compassion. I can be God's agent in increasing the world's supply of these blessings.

The two insights harmonize, singing together a song of Jewish life enriched by the beauty and holiness of ritual practice; a life of deeds infused with God's grace and love, compassion and mercy.

So that terrified bar mitzvah boy received a great gift. The Song by the Sea has intertwined with my life, with its enduring lessons about ritual and ethical beauty.

Rabbi Daniel Pressman has served for thirty years as the Rabbi of Congregation Beth David in Saratoga, California. He was the originator of "Torah Sparks" commentary on the weekly portion for the United Synagogue and has served in a number of leadership roles in the Conservative Movement.

"Who is like You, Eternal One, among the celestials?
Who is like You, glorious in holiness,
Awesome in praises, doing wonders?
You stretched out Your right hand—
The earth swallowed them.
In Your love You have led the people that You have redeemed;
In Your strength You have guided them to Your holy abode."

Exodus 15:11–13

The Song of Moses

Throughout my time as a pastoral leader of a congregation and other faith organizations, the story of Moses has served as a source of wisdom and strength for me, as I seek to lead with the same intent and purpose as did Moses. Moses struggles and leads with a fidelity that is unquestionable. He, like any leader of a congregation, is faced with guiding people through the many trials and tribulations of faith in the unseen but known presence of the Divine even when they doubt, who find themselves lost or rebel against the difficult moral demands of faith.

Moses' faith is based upon a relationship with YHWH whom he knows has been his salvation. Moses knows the power of YHWH to mold reality and to provide a path for salvation based upon steadfast love and kindness. Moses *knows* YHWH because he has *experienced* the presence of the Divine as a great power whose intent and acts originate in steadfast love. Moses experiences the Divine as loyal steadfast lovingkindness which intervened in his own salvation. For Moses, the intent of YHWH's great power has been revealed to be intended for securing the freedom of his own life and the life of his people from oppression.

To *know* God is to know that the Divine is a steadfast, loving presence which acts in history on behalf of each person and all of humanity. As a person of faith and a leader of a congregation, my mission is the same as the Moses of history—to focus on creating awareness of God as *known* in this way to each person who has chosen me to be their pastor or leader.

Moses taught me the purpose and focus of the pastoral call—to speak out that the Divine guides humanity through history and in each person's existential circumstances through steadfast love. My sole task as a pastor is to empower each person to pay attention to the loving voice of the Divine in his or her own heart. My sole task as a teacher is to view human history as the revelation of divine love in the universe. Moses, though many millennia before my time, has always taught me the meaning of purpose of life and the goal of pastoral leadership—not to reach the Promised Land, but to teach and preach that the Promised Land and the power of the Divine is already present in each human life and in the history of the universe.

Reverend Dr. Janet Bregar teaches in the Comparative Religions Department at California State University, Fullerton. She is also the Pastor at Village Lutheran Church at which Ahavat Torah Temple and Sufi Islamic Musallah Tajid are also located. Dr. Bregar is an Ambassador for the Parliament of the World's Religions and is active in many interfaith activities.

And Jethro, the priest of Midian, Moses' father-in-law, heard of all that God had done for Moses, and for Israel, God's people, how the Eternal One had brought Israel out of Egypt. . . .

. . . And Jethro, Moses' father-in-law, came with his sons and his wife to Moses in the wilderness where he was en- camped, at the mountain of God; and he said to Moses: "I, your father-in-law Jethro, am coming to you, and your wife, and her two sons with her." And Moses went out to meet his father-in-law, and bowed and kissed him; and they asked each other of their welfare; and they came into the tent. . . .

. . . And Moses let his father-in-law depart; and he went his way to his own land.

Exodus 18

A Biblical Model of Interfaith Relations
Exodus 18:5–7

I have known for years that interfaith work would be central to my rabbinate. But for much of my rabbinic training, I struggled to find compelling justification for substantive interfaith en- gagement rooted in Jewish tradition before the modern era. Certainly the early rabbis developed models of how to engage with non-Jews, but none of them spoke to the personal experi- ences of transformation I had in my encounters with Muslims and Christians. None of them could account for the fact that my self-understanding as a Jew was deepened through engaging the "Other."

So instead, I drew my inspiration from great 20th century Jewish thinkers like Emmanuel Levinas and Abraham Joshua Heschel to drive my mission of strengthening interfaith understanding and collaboration. But last year, I finally discovered the compelling model of interfaith relations rooted in ancient Jewish tradition that I had been seeking. The model was not from the rabbis; it predated them. The model was in Torah itself.

There are two separate stories in Exodus 18. In the first, Moses relays the wonders of God's deeds to his father-in-law who is so overcome by joy that he blesses the Israelite deity. In the second, Jethro observes the grueling toll leadership takes on Moses and prescribes a model of delegating responsibility. Moses adheres to all of his father-in-law's recommendations. Until last year, I saw these stories in the context of the larger narrative of the people of Israel. The first affirms the power of God. The second tells us how our ancestors made society work.

But last year, these stories became something more personal and more intimate. I saw Exodus 18 as one unified story about the impact two people have on each other through a profoundly trusting and honest relationship. Moses and Jethro are religious leaders representing very different faith traditions. But both men allow themselves and their religious sensibilities to be transformed by their relationship with the other.

Jethro refuses to deny the power he felt when he heard the extraordinary religious experience of his son-in-law. In acknowledging the power of the Israelite God without abandoning his own faith convictions, he expands his understanding of his own spiritual tradition. And Moses takes seriously Jethro's interpretation of God's will for his own people—allowing his father-in-law to transform his own religious leadership and Jewish tradition itself.

This torah speaks to the truths that I have experienced in interfaith work. Moses and Jethro reach divinely-inspired epiphanies because their relationship is defined by trust, reciprocity, respect, mutuality, and openness. For interfaith work to be substantive and meaningful, I believe it must go beyond tolerance and reach these higher levels. When we allow the other to transform us, we create the potential to strengthen not only ourselves but also our tradition.

Rabbi Sarah Bassin was ordained by Hebrew Union College in 2011 and now serves as the executive director of NewGround: A Muslim-Jewish Partnership for Change. Prior to her work with NewGround, Sarah was the program manager at the Center for Muslim-Jewish Engagement where she completed the first comprehensive survey in the field of Muslim-Jewish engagement in North America.

And Moses said to his father-in-law: "It is because the people come to me to inquire of God; when they have a matter, it comes before me; and I judge between a man and his neighbor, and I make known the laws of God and God's teachings." And Moses' father-in-law said to him: "The thing that you do is not good. You will surely wear away, both you, and this people that is with you; for the thing is too heavy for you; you are not able to do it alone. Listen now to my voice. I will give you advice, and God be with you: You represent the people before God, and you bring the matters before God. And you will enjoin upon them the laws and the teachings, and will make known to them the way they are to go, and the practices they are to follow. Moreover you shall provide out of all the people able men, such as fear God, men of truth who hate unjust gain; and set these over them as chiefs of thousands, chiefs of hundreds, chiefs of fifties, and chiefs of tens. And let them judge the people at all seasons; and it will be, that every great matter they will bring to you, but every small matter they will judge themselves; so will they make it easier for you and carry the burden with you. If you will do this thing, and God commands you so, then you will be able to endure, and all this people will also go to their place in peace."

Exodus 18:15–23

You Never Know Where a Good Idea Will Come From

I always loved the passage in Exodus 18 where Moses is kind of hanging around and encounters his father-in-law. I was charmed early on by the idea of the great Moses getting advice from a "gentile" father-in-law about how Moses was likely to wear himself out along with the people.

Only in my more mature years did I come to understand the significance of Jethro urging Moses to restrict his activities and delegate authority for judging to others. It's clear what the biblical author had in mind in general, but what isn't entirely clear is the intent of our author in being so specific about the size and scope of the judges' authority. Of course it is possible that at some point in history these divisions—thousands, hundreds, and fifties—were in fact in place, and that the Torah simply ascribed the origin of that formula to Moses as he responded to Jethro. Who knows?

And who could know that the concept would wind up in a terrifically sophisticated sermon by the great and strange Rabbi Nachman of Bratzlav in the late 18th century. Nachman viewed the world in hierarchical terms and felt that Jethro understood that throughout the world, authority and sovereignty were divided and delegated in a similar way. Indeed for Nachman, or so it has seemed to me, the divisions that Jethro urged Moses to set up were not recommended simply as being fitting as much as they were already in place—that is, the world was divided into those realms of sovereignty no matter what we regular people did. This was the natural order of things. Nachman believed that there were manifest ways in which this was so, and occult ways that we humans could not even know. And he attached "sovereignty" to the word *malchut* (royalty or kingship) which related to a place on the kabbalistic hierarchy emanating from the Godhead. So for Nachman everyone had a measure of *malchut*—the same sovereignty no matter what size community it was over.

I love to think about this idea, and I await the emergence of this Torah portion every year. Its vigor trumps the Ten Commandments for me—a relevant comment since the Ten Commandments are found in this very portion. What is here is a description—not only of the need to distribute power and authority—but to understand the way the world really works. No matter how much we talk and struggle to lead, some things are happening anyway, with or without our hand on the rudder.

William Cutter (Rabbi Bill Cutter), Ph.D., is Emeritus Professor of Literature and Steinberg Emeritus Professor of Human Relations at Hebrew Union College in Los Angeles, where he has taught for forty-six years.

*". . . You have seen what I did to the Egyptians, and how I
bore you on eagles' wings, and brought you to Me. . . ."*

Exodus 19:4

Carried Away

This verse is embroidered on the *tallit* (prayer shawl) that I wore
to my rabbinic ordination in Cincinnati in 2007. I had it embroidered on the *atarah* (collar) in Jerusalem when I lived there
as a rabbinical student with my wife Hope, and our nine month
old son Eli. It recalls my journey to the rabbinate and finding
my peace.

In 1996 I gave myself this *tallit* as a twenty-sixth birthday
gift as if marking the occasion of becoming bar mitzvah times
two. At that time I was wandering in a wilderness of uncertainty.
Three years earlier, I had run away from law school to Israel as a
Sherut La'am volunteer. But at that time I was more confused
than ever: about how to make my living, how best to continue
the Jewish learning I was gleaning from Israel, how I could ever
find such joyful purpose again.

The *tallit* is sometimes compared to an eagle with the
prayerful implication that just as the *tallit* is spread over us like
wings, so, too, might God's sheltering presence somehow hover
over us, keeping us safe. The eagle is likewise a symbol, of the
authority of the law and is also, ironically, the mascot of Boston
College Law School, the school I left. Looking back, the legal
profession had become my *Charan*, the territory I fled. My escape led eventually to the rabbinate.

Once I learned Rashi's squiggly script and terse language, his
commentary on my verse spoke to me and to my journey. Rashi
wrote that other birds shelter their young between their feet but

the eagle carries her young on top of her wings. She has nothing to fear from above.

Like thermal updrafts helping me to soar or rock under my nest, so many people have supported me and taught me to think beyond myself. They have lifted me on their wings. Among them, are the gifted teachers who taught me to stop thinking mainly of myself and to start recognizing the importance of others. I could never have succeeded without Hope and Eli, and the rest of my family, including aunts, uncles, cousins and grandfathers.

There have been all kinds of challenges. There will be more. Yet I have learned to recognize that each challenge is an opportunity to fly faster, higher, stronger. So may it be God's will.

After ordination, **Rabbi Justin Kerber** served as Executive Director of University of Georgia Hillel in Athens from 2007–2009. He has been the Rabbi of Temple Emanuel in St. Louis since 2009. Other than Hope and Eli (sharing a love for food and drink, reading and traveling with Hope and an enthusiasm for *Star Wars*, super heroes, animals, cycling, skating, and swimming with Eli), and besides getting to follow his calling, he is most excited about his newfound passion for playing guitar and singing. The entire family was thrilled to welcome its newest member, Daniel Abraham Kerber, just before Rosh Hashanah, September 2011.

"'. . . And you will be to Me a kingdom of priests, and a holy nation.' These are the words which you will speak to the children of Israel."

Exodus 19:6

Aspiring to Godliness

Although many verses in the Bible speak to me on all kinds of levels, my favorite verse in the Torah is Exodus 19:6: "You shall be to Me a kingdom of priests and a holy nation." The reason I like it is that in my view it articulates the ultimate reason to live as a Jew. As I document in my book, *For the Love of God and People: A Philosophy of Jewish Law*, the Torah describes eight different rationales for living according to Jewish law, and the Rabbis add four more, but ultimately it is the aspiration involved in this verse that is most compelling to me. That is because in the end I think that especially in a voluntaristic society like the United States, where everyone has freedom from religion as well as freedom of religion, if one is going to take Judaism seriously, it must be a matter of personal conviction. To live as a Jew because you want to be part of a people that strives to be godly in its behavior and in its interactions with others and that, as such, strives to make this a better world gives Judaism ultimate meaning to me. It is a goal for which it is worthy to devote my life's energies.

It even affects my day-to-day actions. If I want to be part of a holy people, I need to do the best that I can to make sure that each and every act I do reflects well on God and the People Israel. This is called *kiddush ha-shem*, sanctifying God's Name; the opposite is *hillul ha-shem*, desecrating God's Name. This means, for example, that I must treat all of the help at my place of work or anywhere else with dignity and even kindness, and that

I must drive both safely and courteously. To do otherwise—
especially if I am wearing a *kippah* or am otherwise easily identi-
fied as a Jew—would be to desecrate God's Name and to
undermine my mission and that of all other Jews to strive to be
a holy people.

Rabbi Elliot N. Dorff, Ph.D., is Rector and Distinguished Professor
of Philosophy at American Jewish University, Visiting Professor at
UCLA School of Law, and Chair of the Conservative Movement's
Committee on Jewish Law and Standards. He has written over two
hundred articles on Jewish thought, law, and ethics, and he has edited
or co-edited twelve books and written twelve other books on these
subjects.

*"I the Eternal am your God who brought you out of the
land of Egypt, the house of bondage. . . ."*

Exodus 20:2

A Verse from the Torah
A Personal Choice

The text of the *Kiddush* that inaugurates Shabbat alludes both to
the mystery of creation and the miracle of Jewish history. As
human beings we've been elevated above the beasts; as Jews
we've been shaped by a long record of divine blessings and
curses reflected in our achievements, our misdeeds, and our suffering. That's why the first of the Ten Commandments isn't
about theology but about history. History gives us intimations
of God's presence in time. It sustains the Jewish people and im-
bues it with hope. This discovery has brought me from the
secular perplexity of my early years to the religious faith of my
adult life.

Abraham Joshua Heschel taught that the beginning of faith
is "radical amazement." Contemplating creation fills me with
awe and offers intimations of the Creator. Reflecting in wonder
on Jewish history affirms me in my commitment to my people.
Without ignoring the hardships Jews have endured through
the ages, some of which I experienced as a witness to the
Holocaust, and the questions about God's purpose that arise
from it, I nevertheless cannot but marvel at the survival of the
Jewish people. I'm privileged to live at a time when Jews and
Judaism have again come to play a significant role in human history both in the Diaspora and in Israel.

Whenever I'm asked for an accessible introduction to
Judaism I recommend a book that tells our story. Reflecting on
what has happened to us and realizing that none of the theories

of history that humans have devised explain our endurance and our survival points to truth, albeit an elusive one. It seems, therefore, reasonable to see ourselves as witnesses to the presence of God in the world, not as a reward but for testimony. I feel bidden to lead a life that attests to God's presence in the world and I feel bound by the duty to serve God's creatures. It's a burden more than a privilege, but a glorious calling all the same.

Rabbi Dow Marmur is Rabbi Emeritus, Holy Blossom Temple, Toronto; Senior Fellow, Massey College, University of Toronto; author of five books and editor of two; and columnist for the *Toronto Star* and the *Canadian Jewish News*.

"You shall not murder. You shall not commit adultery. You shall not steal. You shall not bear false witness against your neighbor. You shall not covet your neighbor's house; you shall not covet your neighbor's wife, or his male or his female slave, or his ox, or his ass, or anything that is your neighbor's."

Exodus 20:13–17

Israel's Four Noble Truths

Huston Smith, who wrote the book *The World's Religions*, tapped me into the following notion in his section on Judaism, that the last few of the Ten Commandments constitute not the final word with respect to Western law, but they do lay the foundation on which Western law depends. The first four of this group are judicial axioms; no civilization can survive without them—and none has survived without them. No culture can abide stealing, murder, cavorting with another's spouse (or have one's own cavorted with), and anything less in court than "the truth, the whole truth, and nothing but the truth." To boot, cultures also don't handle unbridled jealousy very well; it usually leads to problems with one or more of the previous four.

This passage speaks to me within its foundational virtue. If the world's religions, if the world's peoples, if the world's powers and principalities would rest their various interests within these four "Western Noble Truths," cede their positions to these simple edicts, I suspect that the vast majority of conflict and poverty would clear up in a year or so. Pending taking this passage seriously, all other religious, legal, and moral/ethical considerations are subsidiary.

Dr. Harold W. McSwain, Jr. is pastor of First Congregational
United Church of Christ in Ocala, Florida, conducts the Central
Florida Master Choir, and is active in human rights issues.

"And you shall not oppress a stranger for you know the heart of the stranger, seeing as you were strangers in the land of Egypt."

Exodus 23:9

Befriending the Stranger

Science fiction author Robert Heinlein was popular during my youth. Originally published in 1961, Heinlein's *Stranger in a Strange Land* brought him lasting fame. It was the fact that my friend Doug was reading this novel during junior high school Spanish class that led to my friendship with him and an appreciation of what it means to be an "alien."

Doug and I attended an affluent (at the time) school district. He was Jewish, and I a "mongrel" Protestant from the other side of town. I attended a Lutheran church, because it was closest to our home. Somehow, in a way lost to the vagaries of time, Doug broke his leg in the eighth grade. As his friend, I volunteered to carry his books as he navigated the school hallways on his crutches. For this simple service, his parents rewarded me with an opulent dinner upon his recovery. In addition, I was to be a guest of honor at his bar mitzvah that year. Well, do I remember the welcome I experienced in temple on that auspicious day!

Reciprocity being what it is, I invited Doug to my confirmation that spring. My parents also treated him to a celebratory meal, and our friendship was sealed in ways most junior high schoolers don't experience.

What does it mean to be an "alien" in an environment which is not one's "own?" In Exodus, the Lord exhorts us to receive and support those who are "strangers in a strange land." We all can be aliens in a foreign land. None of us get out of this world alive, and history teaches us that nothing material belongs to us; nothing is our own.

Thanks to Doug and his family I learned a lasting lesson about acceptance, inclusion and belonging. I took this learning into seminary, out into the world of social work, back into the church and now continuously into ministry.

There are no aliens or strangers—only people connecting and accepting.

Reverend Richard Eddy has been an ordained pastor in the Evangelical Lutheran Church of America since 1995, with twelve years experience as a social worker before completing seminary. He has served several congregations in Upstate New York and in Sweden.

And Moses ascended the mountain, and the cloud covered
the mountain. And the glory of the Eternal One dwelled
upon Mount Sinai, and the cloud covered it six days; and
on the seventh day God called to Moses out of the midst
of the cloud. And the appearance of the glory of the
Eternal One was like a devouring fire on the top of the
mountain in the eyes of the children of Israel. And Moses
entered into the midst of the cloud, and ascended the
mountain; and Moses was on the mountain forty days and
forty nights.

Exodus 24:15–18

Fog or Fire?

Some years ago in a class I was taking, the students were shown
a drawing. When the teacher asked each of us what we saw,
about half of us said it was a beautiful young woman. The other
half of the class said it was an old, decrepit woman. "What?" I
thought, "I need to see that again!" Apparently, the teacher explained, it was a drawing that was an optical illusion. Each of us
was correct in what we saw, and each of us struggled to see
what the other half of the class saw. An optical illusion, indeed.

In Exodus 24:15–18, Moses goes up a mountain to spend
time with God and hopefully, get some answers regarding the
people in his charge. While Moses is walking along, he is envel-
oped in a fog, not that unusual when clouds settle over the top
of a mountain. At the foot of the mountain, the Israelites are
looking up to where Moses has climbed. In stark contrast to the
fog, they see a raging fire!

Here's what speaks to me in this reading: *Moses couldn't see the*
fire for the fog. His followers couldn't see the fog for the fire!

Through the years, when I have gone off to seek God, to get answers from God, I have often found myself walking around "in a fog." I have found myself wandering, sometimes aimlessly, but sometimes very deliberately, trying to find the will of God for whatever situation life had presented me. During these times, I tend to remind God that I have been faithful in following God's plan for my life as best I can, and that this time is no different: I want to know that every step I take is God's will for my life. Unfortunately, I can't always see the "fire" of God (the answers, the Spirit, the Light, the Wisdom, the Glory) because I am so consumed with "fog."

That's when this reading becomes a life lesson: What I have to remember is that the fog is temporary, that the fog is just an optical illusion. I have to remember that the fire of God is right there, just beyond the fog, to illuminate my way.

Reverend A. Keith Mozingo is pastor of Metropolitan Community Church of Baton Rouge, Louisiana, where he resides with his four-legged (Maltese) companion, Mattie. He has a B.A. in English, Spanish, and Bible from Lee University, in Cleveland, Tennessee. Rev. Mozingo was ordained in Metropolitan Community Church in 2000 and has pastored churches in Chattanooga, Los Angeles, and Baton Rouge. He served as Music Director of several churches prior to his ordination. Rev. Mozingo also taught school (English, Spanish) in North Carolina and Tennessee for nineteen years.

"And they shall make Me a sanctuary, and I shall dwell within them."

Exodus 25:8

Becoming the Sanctuary

Throughout all of Genesis our ancestors find God available everywhere. Jacob wakes from his dream in the desert and says, "God, was in this Place, and I did not know. How awesome is this Place." In the wilderness, on retreat, in the quiet majesty of the night sky, God is immediately available.

But in the work-a-day world where laundry has to get done, mouths have to be fed, money has to be earned and deadlines have to be met, God is not so readily present. Instead, like the Israelites who are preparing to enter a new home and build a new society, we have to work harder at it. We have to build a place for God with our own hands.

"Asu li mikdash, v'shachanti bitocham:" Make me a sanctuary, and I will dwell within you. Not in it; not in the work itself, not in the product, not in the tools, but through your work, through intentionality and practice, mindfulness and patience, *you yourself* become the sanctuary in which God dwells.

By using my resources at hand, the tools of my trade, the blessings of my life to do the work of building a meaningful life, I can become that sacred Place within which holiness dwells. This is what the Kotzker Rebbe meant when he said, "God dwells where we let God in."

Every day, I have the opportunity to make myself a sanctuary, a dwelling place for God, just by doing the work of living to the best of my ability. It isn't that we are partners with God in God's project—rather God becomes our partner in our work.

Oh Lord prepare me to be a sanctuary
Pure and holy, tried and true
And with Thanksgiving, I'll be a living
Sanctuary to you.

                                        (Shaker Hymn)

Rabbi Elyse Wechterman has served as spiritual leader and educator at Congregation Agudas Achim, a Reconstructionist community in Attleboro, Massachusetts, since 2001. She has authored numerous articles and stories. Rabbi Wechterman serves on the board of the Reconstructionist Rabbinical Association and is a member of the board of Jewish Family Service of Rhode Island. She is also a regular faculty member of Camp JRF in the Poconos. Rabbi Wechterman lives with her husband and two children.

"And I will dwell among the children of Israel, and will be their God. And they will know that I am the Eternal One their God, that brought them forth out of the land of Egypt, that I may dwell among them. I am the Eternal One their God."

Exodus 29:45–46

Making a Home for God

These two verses serve as the conclusion to several long chapters of detail concerning the construction of the *mishkan*, the portable tabernacle in the wilderness. I love them because they are so direct and simple. Here God declares openly what His whole project has been about. The *whole* project, from the beginning of the exodus, not just the tabernacle. Why did God take us out of Egypt? Because He wanted a home in this world, a place to live, and He felt that we could provide it.

Of course that sense of divine at-homeness was not just things to be measured in so-and-so many cubits, or in where to hang the dyed goatskins. It was about *us*, about the kind of people we were, the kind of community we could become. God senses that Israel is the right people (no, I didn't say the *only* right people . . . I have no way of knowing that!) to make God a home.

While the text seems clearly to be speaking of Israel as a collective and of God's desire to dwell among us, commentators as far back as Philo (20 B.C.E.–50 C.E.) and as recent as the Hasidic masters have also read it as referring to each individual. God wants to dwell *be-tokh* or "inside" each and every one of us, if we will fashion a proper home for God within our hearts. These two readings are not in conflict, but complement and complete one another.

God has taken each of us out of our own private Egypt—whatever it is that enslaves us—and has set us free. Why? Not just for us to have fun, or to do whatever we like. God has set us free in order to become our God, to enter into that relationship of intimacy, love, loyalty, and trust with us. "Becoming" is, by definition, a never-ending process; each of us, throughout time, is called to allow that process to happen. Through us, in us, amid us and our community, God hopes to find a home in this world.

We are ever entrusted with this task of *mishkan*-building. Each generation, each community, every single person. Each of us has to do it in our own unique way, and yet we have to share that work with one another so that the one God, the single One who unites us all, can dwell both within us and among us.

Why does this verse speak so personally to me? Because I see my own freedom as such a precious and yet fragile gift. What to do with that freedom and how to respond to it are among the great questions that pursue me through life.

Arthur Green is a rabbi, scholar, and teacher. He is an interpreter of the mystical and Hasidic traditions for contemporary Jews. Author and editor of more than a dozen books, he serves as Rector of the Hebrew College Rabbinical School in Newton, Massachusetts, which he founded in 2003.

"See, I have called by name Bezalel the son of Uri, the son of Hur, of the tribe of Judah; And I have filled him with the spirit of God, in wisdom, and in understanding, and in knowledge, and in all kinds of workmanship. . . ."

Exodus 31:2–3

The Art of Teaching

This description of Bezalel as having *wisdom, understanding, and knowledge* has become the basis of my teaching philosophy both as a professor and as a rabbi. I began my teaching career believing that the educational process was primarily about conveying information. For me, the first of the three words, *wisdom*, represents a traditional understanding of education in which a teacher pours his/her knowledge into a student, and that student's job is only to absorb and regurgitate. However, I quickly realized that the situations I had faced would not be those that would come before my students. I began to comprehend that the term *understanding*, the second term associated with Bezalel, is a higher level of intelligence related to an ability to apply what was being learned to unique and challenging situations so that I began to teach students how to use their own creativity to transform the wisdom they had absorbed.

I soon began appreciating that the students sitting before me were unfolding, growing, questioning, developing their human potential, and that the education process for them was a sacred pilgrimage. Moreover, my personal sacred journey was being transformed by these interactions as students shared with me their experiences, their observations, and their insights. In gifting me with their *knowledge*, gained outside the classroom, my students taught me to understand this third element applied to Bezalel. Accordingly, I began to view students as fellow pilgrims along life's journey who had something to learn from me and from whom I had much to learn. I expanded my teaching goals to encourage students to realize the importance of their own acquired knowledge. I now endeavor to teach the three levels of intelligence ascribed to Bezalel through the creation of an environment of mutual respect and trust in which students learn from themselves, from each other, and from the teacher. And I end every semester with the following Talmudic statement:

> One learns a great deal from one's teachers;
> One learns more from one's colleagues;
> One learns the most from one's students.

Rabbi Arthur Gross-Schaefer is Professor and Chair of the Business Law/Marketing Department of Loyola Marymount University in Los Angeles. He is also the rabbi of the Community Shul of Montecito and Santa Barbara.

And Moses said to the Eternal One: "See, You say to me, 'Lead this people forward,' and You have not let me know whom You will send with me. And You have said, 'I know you by name, and you have also found favor in My eyes.' So now, if I have found favor in Your eyes, please show me Your ways, and I may know You, and continue to find favor in Your eyes; and consider that this nation is Your people." And God said: "My presence will go with you and I will give you rest." And he said to God: "If Your presence does not lead, do not carry us up from here. For how will it be known that I have found favor in Your eyes, I and Your people unless You go with us, so that we may be distinct, I and Your people, from all the people that are on the face of the earth?"

And the Eternal One said to Moses: "I will do also this thing of which you have spoken, for you have found favor in My eyes, and I know you by name." And he said: "Show me, please, Your glory." And God said: "I will make all My goodness pass before you, and will proclaim the name of the Eternal One before you; and I will be gracious to whom I will be gracious, and will show mercy on whom I will show mercy." And God said: "You cannot see My face, for humankind shall not see Me and live." And the Eternal One said: "Behold, there is a place by Me, and You will stand upon the rock. And it will come to pass, while My glory passes by, that I will put you in a cleft of the rock, and will cover you with My hand until I have passed by. And I will take away My hand, and you will see My back; but My face will not be seen."

Exodus 33:12–23

Insider Information

Moses in the cleft rock (Exodus 33:12–23) has always been one of my favorite stories and one with personal comfort in uncertain times.

In just such a time, when the chips are down for Moses and pressure mounting to lead a difficult people after the trauma of the Golden Calf and the smashed Tablets, Moses would very much like a little insider information as to God's character and God's plan. He's the leader, and he'd like a little more clout with the folks. "Show me your glory," says Moses. "I'd like the folks to know that I've found favor with you."

In a delightful exchange, the LORD says, "All my goodness will pass before you . . . ," with a reminder to Moses that God is autonomous, offering grace and mercy as God so determines, and no one gets to see God's face, not even Moses.

Yet, with a divine kindness, God understands how vulnerable Moses is and that he has the weight of leadership upon his shoulders, and so God "relents," so to speak, and puts Moses into the cleft of a rock. As God approaches, God's hand covers Moses in the rock—Moses cannot see God coming toward him. But only after God passes by do we read this delightful note: God will remove the hand, and Moses will see God's backside.

This has always captured the essence of time for me—we cannot see God in the future, God coming toward us, but only in retrospect, only after God and time has passed us by. Then, we might well say, looking at God's backside, "Ah, so that was the work of God."

Like Moses, we'd all like some insider information. We'd like a leg up on the competition, so to speak. A little more clout with the folks. But such can never be the case. God refuses to become anyone's lapdog. Even as God calls and raises up women and men to lead God's people, not even someone as great as Moses can get insider information. I suspect God realized that Moses, as strong as he was, would have been tempted, like Bilbo or Frodo with the ring of power, to use the glory of God for untoward purposes—a temptation any leader faces.

The passage is, nonetheless, suffused with the assurance of God's goodness and reliability for all of us: "You can trust me because I'm good. I'll go with you, all the way, and I will give you rest."

That's all the insider information we need.

The Reverend Dr. Thomas Eggebeen is an ordained Presbyterian pastor. Dr. Eggebeen, a native of Wisconsin, celebrates forty-four years of marriage to a patient and very wise woman. They have a son in the Peace Corps, Swaziland, and a daughter and her husband in Los Angeles. Dr. Eggebeen has served churches in West Virginia, Pennsylvania, Wisconsin, Oklahoma, Michigan, and California. He has been in the ministry forty-one years. Aside from reading just about anything, cooking is his passion, as well as beachside strolls with his wife. Dr. Eggebeen is "retired," serving as Interim Pastor, Calvary Presbyterian Church, Hawthorne, California.

How Will They Know?

Through the years I have pondered a brief section from the thirty-third chapter of the Book of Exodus. Moses said to God: "If your presence will not go, do not carry us up from here. For how shall it be known that I have found favor in your sight, I and your people, unless you go with us? In this way, we shall be distinct, I and your people, from every people on the face of the earth."

Moses knew that the thing that made them distinct was their relationship with God. They would be just like any other people unless God went with them. And unless they were seen by others as God's people. It was God's presence that set them above every other nation and every other people.

What I ponder is, how in today's society do we communicate that God is with us and we are God's people? When people look at us, how do they know that our God is walking with us? We carry no sign that reads "Jew," "Christian," "True Believer," etc. We wear no outer markings, such as a tattoo, that distinguish us from any other people.

Orthodox Jewish men of the Hasidic community wear broad-rimmed hats, dress in long, black coats, and wear side-curls. Orthodox Christians wear very similar garb. Roman Catholic priests wear clerical collars and carry prayer beads. That, however, is a small minority of us. Unlike certain groups of monks, who shave their heads and wear orange clothing to distinguish themselves from others, most people in the family of Abraham are just ordinary folks living ordinary lives in various cultures around the world.

The Laws of Moses basically define what God expects of us: how we are to treat one another, how we should treat the earth, our responsibilities to society and to God. The teachings of Jesus are based on the Laws of Moses, especially two—to love the Lord your God with all your heart, soul, mind and strength and to love your neighbor as yourself.

Many years ago I learned an old camp song entitled "They will know we are Christians by our Love." It's simple—some may even say simplistic—but I ponder what else really does distinguish us from other people. Love of God, love of God's creation, and love of one another. It sounds so simple, but it proves to be so complex!

Pastor Bob Bock has been the senior pastor of First Christian Church in North Hollywood, California for forty-two years. He has been involved in interfaith dialogues throughout his ministry and was influential in the founding of the Interfaith Food Pantry in Studio City, California twenty-seven years ago. His greatest passion has always been for the welfare of underprivileged children and youth.

*And the Eternal One descended in the cloud, and stood
with him there, and proclaimed the name of the Eternal
One. And the Eternal One passed by before him, and proclaimed: "The Eternal One, the Eternal One, God,
compassionate and gracious, long-suffering, and abundant
in goodness and truth; extending mercy unto the thou-
sandth generation, forgiving iniquity and transgression
and sin; and yet will by no means clear the guilty, visiting
the iniquity of the fathers upon the children, and upon the
children's children, unto the third and unto the fourth
generation."*

Exodus 34:5–7

God's Limitless Love Outshines
Mankind's Sinfulness

I chose this passage because it speaks to me about the intimate
grace-filled interaction between God and our own shortcomings. This passage speaks to me about family and communal
blessings and dysfunctionality. It helps me to find meaning as to
why so many people are blessed and/or suffer through generations of similar experiences, giftedness, maladies, illnesses
and/or diseases at every level of our humanity. This scripture
reminds me that God desires our blessing but often we choose
to remain in our wickedness. Our militant refusal to grow up or
to take charge of our lives invariably influences or infects the
entire family tree for generations to come. It reminds us that we
belong to each other and that our inaction can affect the lives of
untold thousands. On the other hand when we cooperate with
God's will in our lives, countless blessings come our way and
can be passed down through the generations. I have experienced
this truth in my own family's struggles and blessings.

Father Jim Clarke is the Director of Spiritual Formation and chairman of the Spiritual Theology Department at St. John's Seminary. He is also Associate Spiritual Director at the Cardinal Manning House of Prayer for Priests. Fr. Clarke is a popular retreat director and conference speaker throughout the Southern California area and beyond. Fr. Jim received his Masters in Divinity from St. John's Seminary, his Masters in Counseling from Trinity College of Graduate Studies, and his Masters in Religious Education from Fordham University. He also received his Ph.D. in Mythology with an emphasis in Depth Psychology from Pacifica Graduate Institute.

And it came to pass that Moses came down from Mount Sinai. And as he came down from the mountain and the two tablets of the covenant were in Moses' hand, Moses did not know that the skin of his face was radiant since he had spoken with God. And Aaron and all the children of Israel saw Moses and beheld that the skin of his face was radiant; and they were afraid to come near to him. And Moses called to them; and Aaron and all the leaders of the congregation returned to him; and Moses spoke to them.

Exodus 34:29–31

Accepting God's Love

I try to pray when I go out to dinner at a restaurant. I say *try* because I inevitably check over both shoulders to see who may or may not be noticing me. When I feel I'm in the clear I quickly mark myself with the sign of the cross and race through a table blessing. Then I look up to see that no one has caught me praying. Relief.

This differs starkly from Moses who stands beaming from his conversation with the Lord. The people of God fear Moses' holiness, and he has to beckon them. Yet I hope no one sees *my* love of the Lord. How often have I apologized or downplayed my own radiance? On retreats with teenagers, I have stood in front of them and beamed about how much I love God and how thankful I am that I have been called to ministry. Inevitably one of them approaches to compliment me or thank me for my words and I respond, "Aw shucks. You're too sweet." Why am I embarrassed to let my radiance shine?

I find a kinship with the Israelites, wanting to put a veil on the holy. It is easier for me to see God through a veil. Maybe then I do not have to face the toughest reality of all—God loves me. At times, God has shone through my face.

The answer for this lies much in my upbringing. My father hit my mother. He left her. He left my brother and me. That violence cast a shadow on our home. So every time something good happened as a child, I expected this darkness to emerge. I expected this boogeyman to return to hurt us. I loved school as a child but hated the walk home. I remember gripping my house key in between my index finger and middle finger as I walked home from school, prepared to gouge out the eyes of a potential attacker. Despite how wonderful school had been, I always expected my father, the personification of evil for me, to return at any moment.

This passage from Exodus has helped me tremendously over the years. It reminds me that God's love can light up the world. Moreover, Moses' insistence and invitation that people come to him has been an invitation for me. "Come, PJ, let the law of God touch your heart. Come let me teach you that evil does not await around the corner." Or as the prophet Ezekiel proclaims, "I will give you a new heart and put a new spirit in you; I will remove from you your heart of stone and give you a heart of flesh."

Paul J. Shelton, S.J. is a Jesuit scholastic studying for priesthood at the Boston College School of Theology and Ministry. God-willing, he will be ordained a priest in 2014. He took vows of poverty, chastity, and obedience as a Jesuit in 2005. He has taught theology at Marquette University High School in Milwaukee. He holds an M.A. in social philosophy from Loyola University Chicago and a B.A. in History and Classical Languages from Marquette University in Milwaukee. His mother and brother, both of whom he adores, still live in his hometown of Columbus, Ohio.

LEVITICUS

You shall not hate your brother in your heart; you shall surely rebuke your neighbor, and not bear sin because of him. You shall not take vengeance, and you shall not bear any grudge against the children of your people; and you shall love your neighbor as yourself: I am the Eternal One.

Leviticus 19:17–18

From Hatred to Love

On the surface of it, the Torah's demand that we love everyone is absurd. Either you love or you don't. When we love freely and easily we don't need a *mitzvah* (commandment). When we don't, not only is the Torah powerless, but we ourselves feel powerless to make ourselves love. Even worse, if read in context, the commandment to love follows the prohibition to hate suggesting that we are duty bound to love those whom we once hated.

The sequence reads as follows: *Don't hate your brother in your heart. Reprove your fellow. But [and?] do not bear sin because of this! Don't take vengeance or bear a grudge. Love thy fellow as thyself.*

The verses tell a story of fracture. Something happened and you are upset. You shall not hate your brother "in your heart." Don't bottle up that rage; openly express yourself, share your upset. Reprove him!

Then the next phrase cautions: *Do not bear sin!* Be very careful. This may be cathartic for you, but you might just make things worse. Speak your mind, but be careful not to shame the person by reproving her in public. Don't make unfair assumptions or forget your own shortcomings as you point out his.

The text continues: *You shall not take vengeance or bear a grudge.* If you feel hurt, let it go. Don't feed the disconnection by taking revenge. Let bygones be bygones. Let the past sink into irrelevance. And then perhaps you will come to: *Love your neighbor as yourself.*

Love your neighbor as yourself seems then to involve two steps. It begins first with the call to "behave lovingly" with generosity and humility in the wake of inevitable missteps. The text begins by commanding loving deeds and ends by promising rather than commanding love. The feeling of love for one's fellow then doesn't begin the biblical conversation. It appears poignantly at the end of a process, as a result of good relationship practices.

So then, love your neighbor as yourself means: actively love your neighbor because he is *kamocha*—just like you—a person who can mess things up badly. If we will dare to work through the feelings of hurt, reprove gently and listen with humility; if we will let go of rancor and avoid the re-wounding and deepening of conflict with grudges and counter grudges, then we can find our way towards a sustainable and renewable love strong enough to survive the inevitable fractures.

This biblical movement from hatred to love has been enormously helpful to me. I am often asked how I can take the heat of being an openly gay Orthodox rabbi when there is so much real hatred for LGBT people. It helps that I am no longer silent. Since I have begun to speak the truth, my anger has evaporated. There is no need to greet hatred with hatred. Love does not require agreement; it requires empathy. It means that I make myself open to people whose experiences are not mine and I hope that they do the same.

Understood this way, the duty to love requires risking the clarity of the self, because it is the subjectivity of the other that I must fully take in. That is perhaps why the verse ends with, "I am the Lord." I will always be there as an assurance that in your loving openness you will not lose yourself—OR perhaps—If you dare to love, I will hold you over the gap between what you were and what you will become.

Lastly, this musing about love opens up a portrayal of God that is particularly thrilling. God, by containing all perspectives in one, holds all of us together. As Ibn Ezra puts it: Love each other "because I am the One God who authored you both."

Rabbi Steven Greenberg is the Director of the CLAL Diversity Project, Director of Orthodox Programming at Nehirim, author of *Wrestling with God and Men: Homosexuality in the Jewish Tradition,* a scholar-in-residence at Keshet (an advocacy, training, and education organization for LGBT inclusion), a Rabbinical Scholar at Hazon (American's leading Jewish environmental organization), and a co-director of Eshel (an Orthodox LGBT support organization).

Being True to Myself

The Torah verse that has most impacted my life is Leviticus 19:18 which contains the words "You shall love your neighbor as yourself," known as the Golden Rule. But what does it mean to love your neighbor? Toward this end, Hillel, a famous rabbi who died at the beginning of the first century, taught "that which is hateful to you, don't do to your neighbor." This helps us to understand what we should not do to others, but does it really serve as a principle to guide our lives?

It is actually the first half of Leviticus 19:18 that inspires my life. "You shall not take vengeance or bear a grudge against your countryman." While we all would agree that revenge or bearing a grudge are not ways to live our lives, it is the rabbinic interpretation of the verse that provides me a philosophy of life.

Rashi teaches that revenge occurs when "you go to borrow a sickle from someone and they refuse to lend it to you and the next day your neighbor comes to borrow a pick axe. The one who says 'I will not lend you the pick axe, just like yesterday when you wouldn't lend me your sickle' has demonstrated revenge." Bearing a grudge, according to Rashi, occurs when a neighbor fails to lend you a sickle and the next day he comes to borrow a pick axe and you say to him, "Take my pick axe even though you did not let me borrow your sickle yesterday."

Revenge and bearing a grudge come at the cost of our own soul. By refusing to lend something or offering a chastisement during an act of kindness (e.g. sharing) we alter who we are and begin to reflect the ugliness of the person who has wronged us. The Kotzker Rebbe said it beautifully: "If I am me because I am me and you are you because you are you then I am me and you are you. But if I am me because you are you and you are you because I am me then I am not me and you are not you."

When we exhibit revenge or bear a grudge we allow our neighbor to diminish our goodness. In the moment we reflect their ugly action we become like them and lose ourselves. This verse is a constant reminder not to let others define who I am and to always be true to myself.

Rabbi Stewart Vogel is the Senior Rabbi at Temple Aliyah in Woodland Hills, California, where he has served since 1993. He was ordained at the Jewish Theological Seminary and is a Fellow at the Shalom Hartman Institute in Jerusalem. Among his many institutional involvements, he is a Past President of the Rabbinical Assembly Pacific Southwest Region and of the Board of Rabbis of Southern California.

Love Your Neighbor as Yourself

I recently attended a talk by Reverend Terry Hershey entitled "Stop, Look and Listen: The Spirituality of a Crossing Guard." He said that if we do not stop, look and listen then true and lasting beauty passes us by without us appreciating it. Love has to do with beauty, not only the beauty that attracts us to a significant other, but further an infinite beauty that speaks of God and that we cannot hold. The author of Leviticus invites us to strive to see that beauty of God in our neighbor and so, to love our neighbor.

When dwelling on this passage, it occurs to me that it has shaped and challenged my life in profound ways. This passage "Love your neighbor as yourself" has been most challenging on the road. How does driving on the 405 freeway apply to loving of one's neighbor? Is it possible to encounter beauty and so love my neighbor in the midst of horrendous traffic? I would suggest that is why we listen to music in the car because we need to find beauty somewhere. Can we, though, choose to find beauty in that moment of frustration and despair? When we stop, look and listen we don't have to look for beauty and love, they find us.

We must first find beauty in the place where it is at times the most difficult—in ourselves. God has placed beauty in our souls. It is for us to discover it in ourselves and in our neighbor.

Father Tim Klosterman is a priest for the Archdiocese of Los Angeles. He is currently stationed at St. Monica Church in Santa Monica.

And from the sanctuary he shall not go out, nor shall he profane the sanctuary of his God; for the consecration of the anointing oil of his God is upon him: I am the Eternal One.

Leviticus 21:12

Traveling—Without Ever Leaving Home

The conversation went something like this:

"You're going to do what?"

"Yup, I'm going to do it. I'm going to stay in St. Louis till retirement."

"Really? You crazy?"

"Nope—I really like it here . . . I've fallen in love with the people."

As the words left my mouth, I could not help but think of the High Priest of Ancient Israel. It appears that—for all intents and purposes—he was totally confined to The Holy Temple in Jerusalem.

Was his a tragic existence? Could this be my destiny as well? Had I signed on for a form of incarceration—a life sentence in the guise of a life contract?!

Or is it possible that the High Priest is a paradigm? Maybe his existence serves as a balance to the wanderlust that so often afflicts us? Maybe we need not wander from one end of the earth to the other in order to encounter the Almighty? Maybe geography plays no part in our striving for connectedness to the Holy One of Blessing? Maybe we can live lives akin to that of the High Priest? Maybe we can sit in our offices, our studies, and our homes and know that access to Divinity is readily available?

Maybe the life of the High Priest never felt mundane or re-
stricted because he "traveled"—to the most transcendent of
realities—without ever leaving his Temple, his city, his community, and his people?

Maybe. I don't quite know yet. Check back with me in about
twenty-two years. I'll be more than happy to share what I've
learned.

Rabbi Carnie Shalom Rose is the Rabbi Bernard Lipnick Senior
Rabbinic Chair of Congregation B'nai Amoona in St. Louis. He has
participated in some of the most innovative Continuing Rabbinic
Educational Programs including: STAR's From Good to Great,
Kellogg's Management for Jewish Leaders, CLAL's Rabbis Without
Borders, the Hartman Institute's Rabbinic Leadership Initiative, and
the Lead Educators Fellowship Program at the Hebrew University's
Melton Centre for Jewish Education.

And you shall hallow the fiftieth year, and proclaim liberty
throughout the land to all its inhabitants; it shall be a jubi-
lee for you; and you shall return every man to his
possession, and you shall return every man to his family.

Leviticus 25:10

Our Faith and Liberty

From the inception of God's relationship with humanity there is
an understanding of how we are to live in relationship with each
other. Leviticus, the book of duties of priests, or the book of
instructions for leadership, provides this scripture so dear to me
and to our country as an understanding of how we should deal
with those who are indebted to us or captured by us via eco-
nomic, contractual or any other means. Under no circumstances
can one who is in good relations with God perpetuate a condition or circumstance that is oppressive to another human being.

For Americans who are constantly focused on freedom and
liberty, this scripture has been at the forefront of our democracy
and of some of our nation's toughest moments. Our Liberty
Bell has this scripture inscribed, and, as the bell was rung in July
of 1776, it was immediately a symbol of the American
Revolution. With it came the British attempts to capture it, the
British failure, and the crack on the bell. The bell and the scripture on it have become lore.

Later in our history, as the Emancipation Proclamation was
celebrated at the Lincoln Jubilee, there was again the recognition
of this scripture and its special place in America's history. This
scripture continues its effect as we have just opened the Martin
Luther King, Jr. Memorial in Washington, DC, and we again
find ourselves reflecting on the scripture as a nation.

Today it is part of the dialogue on immigration and how we as Christians should respond to the *strangers among us.*

As I find Christians to be the first to say that those who broke the immigration laws should be punished and that anything short of full punishment (deportation) is amnesty, I am stricken by a portion of my brothers and sisters in Christ who have no understanding of Christ and his forgiveness (the Cross being the ultimate Amnesty) and of God's intent on how we should live and love one another. This Old Testament scripture has blessed America because we as a nation have submitted to it. It has not been without struggle or sacrifice, but it has been consistent. This is one of my favorite Old Testament verses . . . in the Book of Instructions for leaders.

Reverend Luis Cortés, Jr. is president of Esperanza, one of the largest Hispanic Evangelical faith-based organizations in the country. In January 2005, Rev. Cortés was featured as one of *Time* magazine's "25 Most Influential Evangelicals." Esperanza, a national network of over twelve thousand Hispanic congregations, faith and community-based agencies, is a leading voice for Hispanics in America.

And I will establish My tabernacle among you, and My soul will not spurn you. And I will walk among you, and I will be your God, and you will be My people. I am the Eternal One your God, who brought you forth out of the land of Egypt, that you shall be their slaves no longer, and I have broken the bars of your yoke, and caused you to go upright.

Leviticus 26:11–13

Knowing God's Heart

I've been teaching a Sunday morning adult class on Leviticus for almost a year. I know that some get lost in the tedious details in Leviticus but I look at it from the broader perspective first. The Creator of the universe, who has rescued His people out of five centuries of slavery in Egypt, brings them out to His holy mountain and gives them the commands of His Law so that they can share in His holiness.

This is amazing! He meticulously outlines every jot and tittle of what He expects from His people from what they eat to where they live because He wants His people to have confidence that they dwell in His favor and share in His holiness. He will be their G-d, they will be His people—that's the refrain throughout Leviticus. What a delight to dwell in the pleasure of the Most High assured of His grace and favor and blessing and kindness and protection against all adversity!

In our modern world, we are so often not only isolated from G-d, but isolated from one another because of sin. In Leviticus, G-d provides for a kind of community built on atonement for sin and reliance on Him and His favor and blessing. Some might look at Nadab and Abihu (Leviticus 10:1ff) and think my thesis doesn't hold. But they deliberately burned "strange fire" before

G-d, provoking His wrath. My point is that Leviticus is about G-d's holiness, not cheap grace, and so there is a religious responsibility to hold fast to the Law that G-d gives.

This understanding has reshaped my perspective of my congregation and my family. We are people who have in common, first and foremost, that we are rescued and redeemed by G-d. When I feel like a failure, and I often do, I know I am forgiven by G-d who desires in His heart to be favorable toward me. When people sin against me, I cannot continue to hold against them what G-d has already forgiven. Christians see this as a forerunner of the theology of Jesus, but back at the mountain, fourteen hundred years prior to Jesus, we have this picture of the true heart of G-d toward His people. It's now having a profound effect on my attitude at worship and prayer, and in sermon writing. I hope I continue to grow in faith to understand it.

Reverend Andrew Smith is a minister in the Lutheran Church–Missouri Synod and a former U.S. Navy Chaplain. He is currently the pastor at Augustana Lutheran Church in Hickory, North Carolina.

NUMBERS

"Have I conceived all this people, did I bear them, that You should say to me, 'Carry them in your bosom, as a nurse carries an infant child to the land which You did promise to their ancestors?'"

Numbers 11:12

Conceiving God

Moses, frustrated by the demands of leading the people Israel, points out to God that he has done nothing to deserve the burden, and uses the language of childbearing and mothering in order to do so. The plain meaning of the verse is clear—to lead is to nurture one's community, to guard and protect it, to help its members grow, painstakingly, into the fullness of their potential as human beings. And, at the same time, God, here, is cast as the mother that, rather than Moses, conceived and birthed this nation.

After the birth of my son, my experience of the Divine, spirituality, and the rabbinate was transformed—unexpectedly and quite radically. Prayer went from feeling transcendent to embodied and grounded with an infant asleep in my arms. Someone I know once described love of one's own children as practice for loving the Divine, but I wonder if it's not the other way around. All those years of connecting with the Beloved have taught me how to offer my heart to someone whose need of me was all the more both urgent and mundane.

There is a sort of radical compassion and service that is demanded in the act of mothering—a compassion that transcends any strict measures of justice. Living that compassion on a day-to-day level, through diaper changes and tantrums, through the sixty-seventh time through a book and the many subversions of my own personal preferences or desires, has an impact. It is easier to love others as I love my own son, desperately, hungrily. It is easier to embody the principles I believe in when the stone of my ego has been worn down, one night-waking at a time. It is more urgent to create good in the world when I think of my legacy to him, or the model I hope to be. Parenting might not be the only way to experience these ways of being, but for me, the impact was extraordinary and profound, even after many years of serious spiritual practice.

I don't know if God mothers, but my own mothering has had an indelible mark on my experience of God.

Rabbi Danya Ruttenberg is the author of the Sami Rohr Prize-nominated *Surprised By God: How I Learned to Stop Worrying and Love Religion*, editor of *The Passionate Torah: Sex and Judaism* and *Yentl's Revenge: The Next Wave of Jewish Feminism*, and co-editor, with Dr. Elliot Dorff, of three volumes on Jewish ethics. Her writing has appeared in numerous anthologies and magazines over the years, and she serves as Senior Jewish Educator at Tufts University Hillel.

And Caleb stilled the people before Moses, and said: "We should go up at once, and possess it; for we are well able to overcome it."

Numbers 13:30

The Faithful Spy, the Land Flowing with Milk and Honey, and the Grasshoppers Who Will Occupy It
A Personal Reflection on Numbers 13

I've always been intrigued by the story and faith of a spy named Caleb. While the Israelites continued to wander in the wilderness, God spoke to Moses and instructed him to send twelve spies—one from each of the tribes of Israel—to scope out the land of Canaan which God had already promised to them.

Moses instructed the spies to search the land and see what it was like, and whether the "people who live there are strong or weak, few or many, and whether the land is good or bad, whether the towns are unwalled or fortified, and whether there are trees or not." Moses' last bit of instruction was simply this: "Be bold."

At the end of the forty days, they returned from spying out the land. As instructed, they gathered all the people together to report to them their findings. "We came to the land to which you sent us; it flows with milk and honey, and this is its fruit. Yet, the people who live there are strong, and the towns are fortified and very large (thought to be twenty feet thick and twenty-five feet tall); and besides, there are descendants of Anak (a race of abnormally large people; Goliath may have been a descendant)."

Despite the rather dismal report, Caleb *insisted* the people "go up at once and occupy it, for we are well able to overcome it!" The other spies didn't see it quite the same way. The fearful said, "We are not able to go up against this people, for they are stronger than we. . . . it is a land that devours its inhabitants, and all the people we saw in it are of great size. . . . we seemed as grasshoppers to them."

Amazing how people can look at the same situation and see it differently. The facts don't change at all. The difference was simply that the majority of the spies were looking through the eyes of fear. Conversely, Caleb was looking through the eyes of faith. The majority saw the obstacles. Caleb saw the possibilities that are available when God is present.

It's easy for us to see walls and giants and respond with fear, all the while forgetting that God has already promised to deliver us and provide for us. May we never forget that "God knows the plans God has for us . . . plans for our welfare and not our harm . . . plans to give us the future we hope for" (Jeremiah 29:11).

Reverend Terri S. Steed is a passionate preacher who believes in the all-inclusive love of God and shares that with "Whosoevers of the World" (John 3:16—all those typically on the periphery of society who are also included in God's all-inclusive love). She resides in Houston with her partner, Kim, and their three puppies, Penry, Jethro, and Phoebe. She serves as the South Texas Network Leader for the Metropolitan Community Church (MCC) and Worship Leader for Resurrection MCC.

"... And there we saw the Nephilim, the sons of Anak, who come of the Nephilim; and we were in our own eyes as grasshoppers, and so we must have looked in their eyes."

Numbers 13:33

To See and Be Seen

As the Israelites make their way through the wilderness, Moses sends out twelve spies, one from each tribe, to scout out the land of Canaan. When they return, the report is at first reasonable—it is a good land but well-defended, and the inhabitants are strong and it will require an effort to overcome them. But as they speak, ten of the twelve lose faith and begin to exaggerate the situation. "They were so big, we looked like grasshoppers in our own eyes, and so we must have looked to them," they report. The people panic, and the two good spies, Joshua and Caleb, cannot convince them to give up their fear and go about the task that God has given them. *Midrash Tanhuma (Shelach 7)* adds a commentary to the text. God says to the evil spies, "You looked like grasshoppers in your own eyes; that I can forgive. But how do you know how you looked in their eyes? Perhaps I made you appear like angels to them!"

As a rabbi and as a person, it is good for me to be reminded that the way I feel about myself does not necessarily correspond to the way I am seen by others.

When I visit patients and families, I enter their room in the name of God. Inside myself, I may feel inadequate to confront what I find there—the parents of a two year old who choked to death, a son who must decide whether to remove his father's respirator, a person so deep in despair that she may be hastening her own death. But I come as God's agent, and I need to keep faith that God is making me appear like an angel to them. It is my job to live up to that and to learn the skills I need to be God's hands in this world.

Rabbi Leslie Bergson is a chaplain for Vitas Healthcare in the Los Angeles area, providing spiritual care to hospice patients. She was ordained by Hebrew Union College–Jewish Institute of Religion in May 1995. Prior to her present position, Rabbi Bergson was University Chaplain and Hillel Director at the Claremont Colleges in Claremont, California.

". . . I am the Eternal One your God, who brought you out of the land of Egypt, to be your God: I am the Eternal One your God."

Numbers 15:41

I Am God, Your God!

Ani YHVH Eloheichem—I am God, Your God. This short section of a verse from Torah, is used in Jewish liturgy as the concluding words to the *SHMA (LISTEN!)* augmented by the word *emet*, the truth. Years ago these words captured my interest, and I began looking up references and found an ancient rabbinic commentary that also wrestled with this statement and its seeming grammatical redundancy. Why not "I am God" *or* "I am Your God?" Why both? The sages gave a speech to God, a list of how God has been there for us—a Warrior at the Sea of Reeds, Source of Inspiration for the poet-king David, Wisdom for Solomon, Comfort as the Ancient of Days for Daniel the prophet—"in each age I will be there for you as you need me to be—I am God, your God!"

You are beyond understanding, transcendent, eternal, yet available, discernable, the possibility for us in our time of life, or time of history. Not the One who makes everything just right for us, or takes our suffering away or gives us surface happiness, but the potential of finding meaning and relevance, energy and hope amidst the narrow place, the deep waters, and the necessary decisions. You are in us as we compose our prayers and songs, journey through our lives reaching for wisdom and, I pray, comfort in the end of our days.

One night in 1994, I chanted the verse over and over and a melody began to form. Within a short time the prayer-song was complete. *Yah Eloheichem Emet.* I recorded it on my first CD,

Heart and Soul, but it has resurfaced in various forms on subsequent recordings since then. I imagine it to be the song I will leave behind as a still small voice when I am gone.

Since that time, this is a verse that I cling to when the truth of love and compassion and meaningful life seems beyond the horizon, unreachable, and perhaps illusory in the face of loss and violence, illness, and our assaulted planet. It is the verse and song that also helps me reclaim and declare over and over again, "I too am here! We matter! The Source of All Life Is, and Is for each person, people, aspect of creation—TRUTH!"

I feel You with me as I write these words, closer than when I began. That is *this* moment's truth. And You will also be here when I lose sight of You, distract myself with the mundane and fear change. I pray Your presence will be with us as we need and will compel us to realize the potential of who we are in the short time we are here. You are the Source of All Life, My Source, That is the truth.

Rabbi Shawn Israel Zevit (www.rabbizevit.com) has many years experience in spiritual and congregational leadership, organizational consulting and training, educational arts, writing, recording, teaching, and performing. He has consulted with numerous corporations, government agencies, non-profit institutions, and faith communities across North America. Rabbi Shawn is also Co-Director with Rabbi Marcia Prager of the Davvenen' Leadership Training Institute (www.davvenenleadership.com) and is a spiritual director and teacher of spiritual direction. He has five CDs of original music and is author of *Offerings of the Heart: Money and Values in Faith Communities* (Alban, 2005), co-editor with Harry Brod of *Brother Keepers: New Essays in Jewish Masculinities* (Men's Studies Press, 2010, www.mensstudies.com), and numerous publications.

Now Korah, the son of Izhar, the son of Kohath, the son of Levi, with Dathan and Abiram, the sons of Eliab, and On, the son of Peleth, sons of Reuben, took men; and they rose up before Moses, with certain of the children of Israel, two hundred and fifty leaders of the congregation, the elect men of the assembly, men of renown; and they assembled themselves together against Moses and against Aaron, and said to them: "You take too much upon you, seeing all the congregation are holy, every one of them, and the Eternal One is among them; why then do you raise yourselves up above the congregation of the Eternal One?" And when Moses heard it, he fell upon his face. . . .

. . . And the earth opened her mouth and swallowed them up, and their households, and all those aligned with Korah, and all their possessions. And they, and all that belonged to them, went down alive into Sheol; and the earth closed upon them, and they perished from among the assembly. And all Israel that were round about them fled at the cry of them, for they said: "The earth might swallow us up." And a fire came forth from the Eternal One, and devoured the two hundred and fifty men who offered the incense.

Numbers 16

Learning About Holiness

While I have held different positions, my only job has been to serve God and teach Torah.

Saying that I serve God can inflate my ego. I try hard, therefore, not to put myself above those with whom I work. At the same time, I try to help my congregants without being servile to them. If I and my fellow rabbis are merely servants of our synagogues, then they are our masters and we are their slaves.

Working out the right balance is the key. How do I remain true to God's will while still being sensitive to the concerns of the Jews in our synagogues? How do I retain humanity and humility while dealing with assertive, demanding people? Aren't there times when I just have to say no?

I find guidance in the story of Korah, who rebels against Moses. While Korah is an evildoer, more troubling are the 250 men who support him. They are "princes of the congregation"—good people who have a seemingly reasonable complaint. "You have gone too far," they say to Moses, "for all the community are holy, every one of them, and God is in their midst."

Aren't these the issues that I face? My leaders too say, "You have gone too far, you have taken on too much." And by implication they might be asking, "Aren't we all holy?" I have wondered if they are not right.

But they are not, because, at the end of the story, the rebels perish. And in studying the commentaries, I have come to understand what the story is about—and what I should expect from myself and others.

I first thought that this is a passage affirming democratic principles. But we already know from Genesis that we are equal in God's sight and created in God's image.

Korah is about *holiness*, a different matter altogether. The rebels claim that we are all holy—regardless of our actions; but the lesson of the story, and of Judaism, is that we are not. If I believe that holiness is conferred upon me automatically, then I am tempted to have a sense of entitlement. I am exempted from responsibility and encouraged to make demands—of God, my fellow Jews, and other people. Holiness understood in this way can only lead to arrogance, pride, and delusions of grandeur.

When my people say that we are all holy, I explain that pure holiness is for God alone, and that even the partial holiness that we can aspire to comes only from obeying God's commandments. ("That ye may remember and do all My commandments and be holy unto your God," Numbers 15:40.) And I remind them that holiness is not a matter of making demands of others but of responding to those demands that God makes of you.

And so I teach the story of Korah frequently, using it as a reminder that I must always apply the same standard to myself that I apply to others: I am no more holy than anyone else, and such incomplete holiness as I might claim can only come from the commandments that I do and not the noble principles that I proclaim.

A Reform rabbi, **Eric Yoffie** was ordained at Hebrew Union College–Jewish Institute of Religion in 1974. He has served congregations in Lynbrook, New York and Durham, North Carolina. From 1996 to 2012, he served as president of the Union for Reform Judaism, the umbrella body of Reform synagogues in North America.

*And the children of Israel journeyed, and they encamped
in the plains of Moab across the Jordan at Jericho. And
Balak, the son of Zippor, saw all that Israel had done to
the Amorites. And Moab was alarmed because that people
was so numerous; and Moab was overcome with dread because of the children of Israel. . . .*

*. . . And Balaam rose up in the morning, and saddled his
ass, and went with the princes of Moab. And God's anger
was kindled because he went; and the angel of the Eternal
One placed himself in the way as an adversary against
him. Now he was riding upon his ass, and his two servants
were with him. And the ass saw the angel of the Eternal
One standing in the way, with his sword drawn in his hand;
and the ass turned aside out of the way, and went into the
field; and Balaam beat the ass, to turn her back onto the
way. . . .*

*. . . And Balaam went with Balak, and they came to
Kiriath-huzoth. And Balak sacrificed oxen and sheep, and
sent them to Balaam, and to the princes that were with
him. And it came to pass in the morning that Balak took
Balaam, and brought him up into Bamoth-baal, and he
saw from there a portion of the people.*

Numbers 22

The Testimony of Balaam's Ass

In the fanciful narrative of Balaam and his donkey, I find this
particular story both encouraging and incredible. In the story,
Balaam is summoned by messengers to appear before King
Balak of Moab in order to curse the Israelites. But there is a rub

in the story. While it doesn't say that Balaam wanted to go before the king, it implies that he did. Maybe he was lured by the promise of riches and wealth. Maybe he thought doing a favor for a king would be good for him down the road. Ultimately he goes with the messengers. On his way, he encounters some trouble with his donkey.

What I enjoy about this passage is not so much King Balak's surprise that Balaam blesses Israel later in Numbers 23, but rather how the faithfulness of Balaam is told in such an imaginative way. If we were to assume this story was real, can you just imagine, after beating your donkey to have it turn and ask, "Why are you beating me?" While the text doesn't explain Balaam's surprise, I'd have fallen off my ass (so to speak) were that to happen to me. And if that weren't enough, after the donkey speaks to him, Balaam's eyes are opened to an angel standing in front of him with a drawn sword in his hand. Then, the angel chastises him for beating his donkey, the donkey that had actually saved his life by not obeying Balaam's commands.

This, after all, is the main crux of the story. Balaam learns to listen to God and to know that whatever his original intentions were, he'd better do exactly as the Lord says or he'll die. What I like about the story is how Balaam keeps his composure throughout this magnificent ordeal. To me, this shows an incredible reflexive faith.

As I encounter God and experience faith, this story teaches me the value of integrity. It teaches me the importance of being faithful to my call both in the pulpit and out of it. And, it teaches me that whatever fantastic surprises await me in ministry, I should always trust that God will reveal to me exactly what I need to know, say, or do—and if I fail to follow my faith, to not be surprised if God uses extraordinary measures to get my attention.

The Reverend Dr. David C. Bocock is the pastor of the Cresskill Congregational Church, United Church of Christ, a liberal parish in the suburbs of northern New Jersey.

***Then drew near the daughters of Zelophahad, the son of
Hepher, the son of Gilead, the son of Machir, the son of
Manasseh, of the families of Manasseh the son of Joseph;
and these are the names of his daughters: Mahlah, Noa,
and Hoglah, and Milcah, and Tirzah.***

Numbers 27:1

The Power of Relationship

They had no power save for themselves. In their world, strength
and property passed from father to son. Their father had died.
They were only daughters. From whence would their help
come? How could they guarantee their future, their family name,
without land to call their own?

*Tikravna b'not Zelophahad—The daughters of Zelophahad drew
near . . . Mahlah, Noa, Hoglah, Milcah, and Tirzah.*

These young women must have realized that they needed to
take action and so they approached authority and asserted
themselves in a way not familiar to the biblical culture and certainly not to the Israelite people as they made their way through
the wilderness toward the Promised Land. What gave them the
strength to approach Moses?

The use of the verb describing what they did—drawing
near—and the explicit listing of their names is what intrigues
me. I am drawn into the drama to discover how they will assert
themselves as women and as members of the Israelite community.

The specific use of the verb *tikravna*, to draw closer, illumi-
nates our understanding. Its core meaning also makes up the
Hebrew word for sacred offering to the Divine, *korban*. In bringing the strength of their bonds with each other, they invoked

the presence of God into the process as well. To draw near means to expose vulnerability while becoming closer. With whom did they first draw near? With one another. It was through the strength of their own relationship which allowed them to leverage their power to bring themselves closer to Moses and to God. They did not know how Moses would react to their assertion that their father's name not be lost just because he had no sons.

"Give us a holding among our father's kinsmen!" is what they declare forcefully and clearly to Moses.

Not only does Moses feel the need to consult with God before passing judgment but the meaning of the word—*tikravna*—and its inherent connection to a sacred offering bind what the daughters are doing with a sacred purpose.

The daughters of Zelophahad teach us the power of relationship. All of their names are there. The approach is through relationship, human and Divine. For me, this biblical tale is another reminder of how we cannot change our destiny or the future alone. We need one another. Recognizing each person for the humanity and strength he or she brings allows each of us to assert a power together to secure justice and to draw near to one another with the sacred intention of guaranteeing a future for ourselves and those who come after us.

Rabbi Elaine Zecher has served as rabbi at Temple Israel, Boston since 1990. She chairs the Worship and Practices Committee of the Central Conference of American Rabbis, was a member of the Editorial Committee for the new prayerbook for the Reform movement (*Mishkan T'filah*), and now chairs the Machzor Advisory Group for the Reform High Holiday Prayerbook currently being developed.

"The daughters of Zelophahad are right in what they say; you shall indeed let them possess an inheritance among their father's brethren; and you shall pass their father's inheritance on to them. . . ."

Numbers 27:7

Bending the Will of God

For me there are two important lessons that can be gleaned from this verse. One addresses a paradox that exists in my life. This paradox is the belief that while God does communicate with humanity, I have no tools to understand either the timing or the content of this communication. When the daughters of Zelophahad raised their voices in protest, I am not sure if anyone who heard this protest imagined that God would not only answer them but answer them with the resounding words, "The daughters of Zelophahad are right in what they are saying." All too often our lives are accentuated by prayers to God that seem to remain unanswered, or at least, prayers whose answer is not discernable by us. But there are sometimes moments in our lives when the fog of divinity becomes clearer, when God's voice attains a clarity that is usually lacking. It is in these rare moments of clarity that any rationalistic understanding of Judaism that I may have takes a back seat to what I understand to be a faint echo of God's revelation.

The second lesson of this verse for me is that there are rare moments when humanity can bend the will of God. After hearing that they would not inherit their father's land, the daughters of Zelophahad argued against God's law. For a Jew who believes that God's word is immutable, this act borders on heresy. On the other hand, for a Jew who believes that humanity is not a totally silent partner in the human-divine relationship, the behavior of the daughters of Zelophahad is both inspiring and frightening. For me this verse is inspiring because here is an example from the Torah of human beings who convince God that the law should be different than originally intended. But it is also frightening because how are we to know that our will is acceptable to God?

This is one of the great challenges that I face daily. How am I able to accept the word of God, yet also acknowledge that sometimes I wish that it were different?

Rabbi Michael Pitkowsky is the Rabbinics Curriculum Coordinator at the Academy for Jewish Religion in New York. He is also an adjunct instructor at the Jewish Theological Seminary of America. He blogs at www.MenachemMendel.net/blog.

The one lamb you shall offer in the morning, and the other
lamb you shall offer at dusk.

Numbers 28:4

The Most Important Verse in the Whole Torah

What do you think is the most important verse in the whole
Torah? I would vote for *Bamidbar* (Numbers), chapter 28, verse 4.

In the introduction to the *Eyn Yaakov*, it says that Rabbi
Yochanan ben Zackai had three disciples, and that he asked
them which verse they considered to be the most important
verse in the Torah. One said, "The *Shema*." Another said, "Thou
shalt love thy neighbor as thyself." And one said this verse,
"You shall offer one lamb in the morning and one lamb you
shall offer in the evening." Rabbi Yochanan said, "I agree with
this one."

Why?

How could Rabbi Yochanan ben Zackai have chosen this
verse about the importance of daily sacrifices as the most
important verse in the entire Torah? That goes against everything we know about Rabbi Yochanan. He was the one who
redefined Judaism after the fall of the Temple. He was the one
who taught that prayer and kindness are as precious to God as
sacrifices are. How then could he have chosen this verse as the
most important in the whole Torah?

This is what I think he meant. "The *Shema*" and "Love thy
neighbor as thyself" are important teachings. There is no doubt
of that. But they are generalities. The real test of our sincerity is
if we demonstrate our commitment every single day. That is
why we say of someone who goes bowling every week or who
plays bridge every single Thursday that they do so "religiously."
What Rabbi Yochanan was teaching us is that if you are serious

about the Jewish way of life and about serving God, you must do something specific, and you must do it regularly. This is why this passage that speaks of making an offering to God every single morning and every single evening gets his vote—and mine as well—as the most important verse in the whole Torah.

Rabbi Jack Riemer is a guide to many rabbis. He is the editor of *The World of the High Holy Days*, of *So That Your Values Live On: Ethical Wills and How to Prepare Them*, and of *Jewish Reflections on Death*.

DEUTERONOMY

Observe the Sabbath day, to keep it holy, as the Eternal One your God commanded you. Six days you shall labor, and do all your work; but the seventh day is a sabbath to the Eternal One your God, in it you shall not do any manner of work, you, nor your son, nor your daughter, nor your male slave, nor your female slave, nor your ox, nor your ass, nor any of your cattle, nor your stranger who is within your gates; that your male slave and your female slave may rest as well as you. And you shall remember that you were a slave in the land of Egypt, and the Eternal One your God brought you out from there with a mighty hand and with an outstretched arm; therefore the Eternal One your God commanded you to keep the Sabbath day.

Deuteronomy 5:12–15

Remember the Sabbath Day, to Keep It Holy

Growing up in Colorado in the 1960s I did not have a deep sense of "Sabbath," but I do recall the blue laws that meant no businesses were open on Sunday. In that predominantly Christian community, there seemed to be an agreed upon understanding that Sunday should look different from other days of the week, reserved for certain activities like church and family meals, exclusive of things that seemed too much of commerce or triviality. At that time my parents even debated as to whether we children should go swimming or to the local movie theater on a Sunday! The day was understood to be set aside.

In the congregation I now serve, forty years later, an altogether different reality exists as families now spend Sundays at swimming or hockey practice, off at tournaments or heading to the mall. I work hard to cultivate a sense of "setting time apart," of being intentional about spiritual rest and replenishment, but

I swim against a cultural current that shows little sign of abating. But daily I see the painful results of these choices in bodies that are fatigued and spirits that are brittle, marriages and families with unmanageable levels of stress, communities where people become strangers to themselves and each other as individuals move at break-neck speed to do, to accomplish, to compete, to stay another step ahead.

In my own life I have come to see that without intentional rest I dishonor the Holy and I show disrespect for my own body and spirit, my relationships, my environment. Without carving out quiet space, meditative space, healing space in the crush and press of my ministry and daily living I would be sucked dry, mere bones like Ezekiel's vision, cut off from all that is holy and life-giving. My commitment to Sabbath rest has come from watching colleagues and friends reach burn-out, and I have seen how my own weariness can lead to the worst kinds of idolatries and destructive patterns. The commandment to preserve Sabbath may be much less for God's sake than for our own.

Each time I slow my pace, immerse myself in the delights of breath and quietude I keep finding my way back to that sacred source in which I truly live, move and have being. There is such joy and peace to be found there, I cannot imagine life without it. Frankly, I cannot imagine God without it. Be still, my soul, and know.

The Reverend Dr. Mary E. Westfall has been ordained for nearly twenty-five years, serving in both Presbyterian Church (USA) and United Church of Christ settings. For nearly a decade she was a university chaplain and has a deep commitment to ecumenical and multifaith work and worship as well as a passion for sustainable living. She now lives in New Hampshire with her partner of nearly thirty years with whom she has two young adult children.

The Meaning of *Shomer Shabbat:*
An Understanding of Deuteronomy 5:12

The term *Shomer Shabbat* (guarding the Sabbath) owes its biblical origins to Deuteronomy 5:12: *Shamor et haShabbat* . . . "Observe the Sabbath Day." Over time, this would refer most specifically to a Jew who observes the laws and rituals of Shabbat; from Sabbath preparation through its conclusion, in the synagogue and at home.

The biblical imperative, however interpreted, may not be sufficient to compel much Shabbat observance from amongst moderns.

Perhaps, though, the understanding of the Sfat Emet (Yehuda Leib Alter, a late 19th century Hasidic master) can aid us.

The Sfat Emet asked, "Why the use of the word *shomer?* What are we guarding exactly?" He notes that, because the Shabbat graces each Jew with an additional soul (*neshama yetera*), a good deal more of us is present on the Shabbat than normal; we are literally doubled, and require double the protection. *Shomer Shabbat* for the Sfat Emet has the Jew guarding the Shabbat, and no less, the Shabbat protecting the individual Jew.

The Sfat Emet's interpretation suggests how deeply personal the Sabbath is—personal in the sense that we are (potentially, if not actually) different on Shabbat: more, not in size, but in spiritual capacity and receptivity.

I usually remain oblivious of this on Shabbat. Occasionally, however, I manage to catch a glimpse of this doubleness—in the glancing awareness of mortality, mostly. The rapid passing of time, of life, mine in particular, is frightening; it can be galvanizing.

Here, then, is how I see the Shabbat as "protective," indeed, galvanizing: it reminds me how precious life is, how the best way to live is to have one day for pause, for reflection, for perceiving differently. All so that I—that we—may appreciate that to be counted among God's creatures, to have a chance at all of this—life, love, meaning, joy, wonder, awe, suffering, too—even if only for a terribly brief moment, is a privilege.

For me, to acquire such knowledge, it's more than worth protecting and observing the Shabbat, notwithstanding the episodic nature of the fuller experience. I figure, the more I protect, the more regular and deeper is the experience, not only of the Sabbath, but of God and of the sacred.

John Moscowitz is Senior Rabbi of Holy Blossom Temple, Toronto, Canada. His blog "From Jane Fonda to Judaism" can be found at www.rabbijohnmoscowitz.blog.com.

Hear, O Israel: The Eternal One is our God, the Eternal One is One.

And you shall love the Eternal One your God with all your heart, and with all your soul, and with all that you have. And these words, which I command you this day, shall be upon your heart; and you shall teach them diligently to your children, and shall talk of them when you sit in your house, and when you walk by the way, and when you lie down, and when you rise up. And you shall bind them for a sign upon your hand, and they shall be for frontlets between your eyes. And you shall write them upon the doorposts of your house, and upon your gates.

Deuteronomy 6:4–9

Oneness

There is really one verse in the Five Books that speaks to me personally above all others. This verse, in my opinion, sums up the Torah. It describes the mission of the Jews as emissaries of G-d in spreading the ideal of monotheism to the world. The verse comes from Deuteronomy, chapter 6, Verse 4:

Shema Yisrael Hashem Elokeinu Hashem Echad—Pay Heed, *People of Israel, G-d, Our G-d, G-d is One.*

What is meant that "G-d is one?" Why does the verse state that only Israel should pay heed?

The word unity, in my estimation, means there is nothing in the universe, no one thing that is distinct from G-d. When I learn a verse in Torah and read commentary, I internalize the lesson through intense study. My intellect is served through my effort. G-d, however, *is* intellect. That is, one cannot separate G-d into constituent parts affected by outside influence. G-d is an all encompassing being and that is the essence of His unity.

When I view the natural wonders of the universe as did Abraham our forefather thousands of years ago, I come to one conclusion. My rational mind and my sense of spirituality bespeak of "oneness." Mere observation brings me to the conclusion that in spite of a diverse universe, there is only One force controlling it, managing it, and keeping it all in synchronized balance. This is G-d, the G-d of humanity, our G-d.

But what does it mean when I declare that G-d is our G-d? Do I believe that a declaration of uniqueness is exclusionary? Quite the contrary, our G-d means that I, as a rabbi, have a responsibility to educate the world on the essence of unity and the method to internalize the message that oneness is synonymous with the Creator.

I am daily inspired by the prophet Zechariah's declaration. He prophesized about Messiah and through his prophetic vision determined that there is but one global consciousness that would bring peace to mankind. He declared that on that day, not only will G-d be understood by mankind as the one force controlling the Universe, but that His essence of being, His name, will be synonymous with Unity. I have made it my life's mission to teach that ideal to my own people and to inspire those I encounter, whether Jew or non-Jew, that the effectuation of this realization will lead to world peace and serenity.

Rabbi Asher Krief is semi-retired, serving part-time in a congregation in New Jersey.

Love in Action

"Ve'ahavta—you shall love!" We are commanded to love God with our whole heart, our full essential self and our entire strength. This is the greatest commandment: total commitment. Samuel David Luzzatto, a 19th century Italian scholar, poet, philosopher, and Bible commentator, taught that this commandment is not separate from others but the underlying principle of them all.

When I recite *"Ve'ahavta!"*—I fill with trust. I renew my willingness to step forward into the world with my whole self not leaving behind my fearful or self-conscious parts. *"Ve'ahavta!"* requires my complete relatedness to self, others and God. I experience my fullness, commitment and courage to meet the unexpected.

Our rabbinic sages taught that all true loving is an expression of joyful and creative gratitude (*b. Yoma* 86a). I am deeply grateful for the gifts of life energy, love, and community that exist in the world. For without them, we could not fulfill the commandment *"Ve'ahavta*—you shall love!"

I am thrilled each morning as I say *"Modah ani*—Thank you God" that I have a new opportunity to bring my love, vitality and creativity fully into the world, to direct my attention and intention towards service and the continuing process of love-in-action and to remember each day the primary importance and essence of loving: *"Ve'ahavta!"*

Rabbi Nancy E. Epstein, MPH, MAHL, is a Reconstructionist rabbi and Associate Professor of Community Health and Prevention at the Drexel University School of Public Health. She formerly served as the Director of Congregational Relations for the Jewish Reconstructionist Federation, as Legislative Committee Director for two Texas legislative committees, as a public interest lobbyist and a grassroots community organizer.

Acting Now for the Future

The verses from the Torah that speak to me in a personal (and professional) way come from Deuteronomy 6:4–9. In this passage, the Israelites are being reminded how important our relationship with God is. If we were to take these verses completely to heart and live them out in ALL of our actions, the world would be a much better place. If we remembered to love God with all our being and showed that love for God to our neighbors, there would be less conflict in the world. This respect for each and every human being would lead us to peace and hopefully to act against hunger, poverty and disease around the world.

These words also remind us how vital our role is in passing on our faith to our children and the future generations. These are actions we are called to do everywhere we go and at every time—not just at church on Sunday mornings! Youth are experiencing so many demands in their lives and upon their time. It is increasingly more important than any other time in history for us to share our faith so that children and youth can grow in their own relationship with God.

I feel one of the reasons I am a pastor today is because my mom, my aunt, my pastor and many other caring adults shared their faith with me. I didn't always want to become a pastor, but my faith always served as a great source of strength and comfort for me—as well as a guiding light in difficult situations. This was all because of the gift that was shared with me by the adults in my life who took it upon themselves to spend some time with a little boy.

After a nine year career in the Texas business world, **Reverend Michael Widner** felt the call from God and attended Luther Seminary in St. Paul, Minnesota. He has been involved in youth ministry for over twenty years and has been an ordained pastor for nine years. He currently serves in a regional yet rural Lutheran congregation in southeast Nebraska, which offers exciting and unique opportunities for ministry with youth and adults.

. . . And you say in your heart: "My power and the might of my hand have gotten me this wealth." But you shall remember the Eternal One your God, for it is God that gives you power to get wealth, that God may establish God's covenant which God swore with your fathers, as it still is this day.

Deuteronomy 8:17–18

An Eye Toward Thankfulness

When Israel was wandering through the wilderness, and anticipating the joy of the Promised Land, Moses reminded her,

> *"You may say to yourself, 'My power and the strength of my own hands have produced this wealth for me.' But remember the Lord your God, for it is He who gives you the ability to produce wealth."*

Deuteronomy 8:17–18

Like most Americans, I was trained with the ideals of Manifest Destiny. Work hard, achieve, and receive the credit. Fail to achieve, and internalize blame. We are the masters of our domains, and God helps those who help themselves. But meditating on the generous character of God quoted above, frees me from such a trap.

In one form or another, this trap usually takes the form of navel-gazing. We long to be recognized as the source, the ultimate power behind all our success.

In my life, our American ideals have incited pride in "my power and the strength of my own hands." As a youth, the pursuit was basketball. In college, the pursuit was education. As a pastor, the pursuit is dazzling programs and slick sermons. Why? Not so much for the joy of pursuing excellence for the glory of God, but for the joy of being recognized as wonderful.

Alternatively, when those sermons are boring or those programs are duds, the overwhelming feeling is envy, pride's wicked cousin. Why can't I be efficient and effusive, more like the pastor on the other side of town? More navel-gazing.

Deuteronomy 8:17–18 frees me from such idolatry. God has granted different gifts and abilities. It is our responsibility to steward them, but He is creator, provider, and sovereign distributor. He has given us the abilities to produce wealth. He has given me the abilities to produce either superb or mediocre programs and sermons.

Such a perspective lifts our gaze toward heaven. Both in our accomplishments and our weaknesses, we are freed from the deception, "I am the Master of my domain." Remember the Lord, for He has given us the ability.

It seems to me that, to have no one but self to thank, is utter loneliness. Because knowing God as sovereign provider frees us from individualistic pride, self-loathing, and envy, it also reminds us that we have a generous and loving God to thank. Regardless of success or failure, riches or poverty, health or sickness, Deuteronomy 8:17–18 invites us to look heavenward and with thanksgiving.

It was among the very first verses I memorized, and as a young Christian, it affected me profoundly. Many years later, it wards off loneliness, girds me with strength, and fosters a spirit of gratitude.

Adrian Boykin lives in Lafayette, Colorado, with his wife Susie and two boys, Elijah and Silas. He serves as pastor for Calvary Bible Church's Erie Campus. He is passionate about helping people know God personally and engage their communities holistically.

*Justice, justice you shall pursue, that you may live, and in-
herit the land which the Eternal One your God gives to
you.*

Deuteronomy 16:20

Justice, Justice You Shall Pursue

Justice, these days, is sexy. One might think that justice would be
happening everywhere as a result. The command in Deuteronomy
16:20 which says *Justice, Justice you shall pursue* makes this hot topic
seem so simple, but we see injustice everywhere. In truth, the
pursuit of justice is deeply complex.

As we seek to unpack the intricacies of this seemingly easy di-
rective, we can begin with the words themselves. In Hebrew, there
are only two words in this three-word instruction: *justice* and *pursue*.

The word *justice* in Hebrew comes from the root meaning
righteousness or *integrity*. In English, we equate these words with
the scales of justice—balance, equality or fairness. *Integrity* as a
translation makes sense because it means balance and equality
between the external action and an internal belief. Justice is
about weighing and balancing all things internal and external,
local and global, needed and desired, hoped for and feared,
merited and guaranteed. Achieving equilibrium is not passive
but it is still, calm, measured and steady.

The Hebrew word for *pursue* comes from the root which
means *chase* or *follow*. In English we equate pursuit with such
disparate, yet passionate, ideas as in "hot pursuit" or pursuing
the object of one's desires like the pursuit of happiness, a
dream, or one's studies. There is an understanding of persis-
tence and challenge, commitment and rigor.

There is a great deal of tension within this text. Justice contains within it a dynamic tension between stillness concurrent

with power. Adding to that oppositional force is the repetition of this teetering word *justice*. It is said twice as if to represent the scales themselves on which all things struggle to stay poised.

I recently spoke with a man who is very active in his pursuit of justice. He spoke of a friend who recently said, *Buddy, do less!* To which this man replied, *I will do less, when you will do more.* The give and take of the Deuteronomy verse lives beyond each of us in the connections between us as well.

This is the brilliance and the beauty of this half-verse of Torah. What seems to be simple is truly quite complicated. We know in our hearts how hard it is to pursue justice, and we see it in the words of the text. And this is why I love it. I think of it when I go for a run and I try to keep my breathing slow while my body moves fast, and I remember the call to justice. When I debate getting more done or taking the time out for rest, and when I encounter any one of life's push-pulls, I remember this call to justice.

Justice, justice you shall pursue calls me to live in the graceful balance and the dynamic tension between acting and thinking, between hate for suffering and love for the sufferer, between devastation and inspiration, between being overwhelmed and being inspired to wake up tomorrow and continue the struggle which is the undercurrent of life.

Rabbi Rachael Bregman serves at The Temple in Atlanta where she heads up Open Jewish Project for Atlanta's young adults. As a justice junkie, Rabbi Bregman served as the Soup Kitchen coordinator at Hebrew Union College in New York City, did community organizing with Jewish Community Action in Minneapolis, taught for Teach and Tour in Kampala, Uganda, was an American Jewish World Service Kol Tzedek Fellow, and currently sits on the board of the Jewish Community Relations Council in Atlanta as well as 10 Partners innovation collaboration and is co-chair of Reform Jewish Voices–GA.

And it shall be, when you come close to war, that the priest will approach and speak to the people.

Deuteronomy 20:2

When We Come Close to War

Having served as a Chaplain in the United States Army Reserve for over thirty-two years, this verse has always been near and dear to my heart. I appreciate the recognition, even thousands of years ago, that soldiers preparing to go into battle need and deserve religious support. Chaplains today, just like priests in the *Tanach*, offer comfort, encouragement, a listening ear and a caring presence.

Judaism is not a pacifist tradition. We believe not only in the right, but the obligation to self-defense. If someone is seeking to kill you, we read in the Talmud, "rise up earlier and kill him first" (*Sanhedrin* 72a). We hope and pray and work for a Messianic age, a time of universal peace and well-being, but, until that blessed day arrives, we must also recognize the importance of a well-trained army to defend our people and our way of life.

We are adjured in Psalms (34:14) to seek peace and pursue it, and prayers for peace are a major focus of our liturgy. It was King Solomon, whose very name comes from the root *shalom*, meaning peace, who built the Holy Temple in Jerusalem; this honor was denied to King David, the triumphant warrior.

While war may at times be necessary, as Jews we are taught never to rejoice in the suffering of our enemies. At the Passover Seder, we spill a drop of wine from our cups, symbol of rejoicing, as we recall the ten plagues. The plagues were a necessary part of our journey towards liberation, yet our celebration is muted.

Chaplains are non-combatants—we do not carry weapons, we are not trained to fight. We are there to minister to the religious needs of the troops, and, as such, we are an essential part of the military force. No one likes war; no one wants war. No one prays for peace with more fervor than the soldier who stands ready to lay down his or her life for our country. Yet I am not a pacifist. I believe that there are times when war is justified. War is always a horrible tragedy, but it is not necessarily immoral.

I am proud to consider among my many identities as wife, as mother, as rabbi, as teacher, as friend, yet another—as an American Soldier. When our country determines that the time has come to take up arms and go to war, our Jewish soldiers need to have rabbis who are trained and ready to deploy alongside them, to be there to offer spiritual direction. I am proud to be among those who have the incredible honor and privilege to be with them on their journey—when we come close to war, I pray that my words will inspire and comfort those to whom I speak.

Rabbi Bonnie Koppell is a Rabbi at Temple Chai in Phoenix. A 1981 graduate of the Reconstructionist Rabbinical College, she has served for over thirty-three years in the United States Army Reserve. She is the Command Chaplain of the 63d Regional Support Command and holds the rank of Colonel.

And so shall you do with his ass; and so shall you do with his garment; and so shall you do with every lost thing of your kinsman, which he has lost, and you have found; you must not remain indifferent.

Deuteronomy 22:3

You Must Not Remain Indifferent

This has been my favorite verse in the Torah for as long as I can remember. And I do remember, as a college student thirty years ago, the first time I picked up the Bible to read it on my own. It was the same semester that I met Elana (then my girlfriend, now my wife) and God (I was clearly in the mood for love!). Reading scripture on my own, in English, hit me with a force beyond description. I was thrilled by the drama and the pageantry, elevated by the wisdom, challenged by the vision of a just, compassionate and righteous society, a vision yet to be implemented.

Then I read these staccato words. In the middle of a paragraph which speaks of our obligation to restore lost items to our fellow (the Torah terms him your brother!), how we are to inconvenience ourselves to return lost property or clothing or livestock, we are then instructed *"lo tukhal le-hitalem"—you must not remain indifferent.* If you were looking for a three word summation of the entire Torah, that would be it.

I have tried throughout my rabbinic work, as a husband and father and friend, not to allow myself to be indifferent. When I saw the exclusion and marginalization of GLBTQ people, I didn't let myself remain quiet. When I fathered a boy who struggles with autism, I didn't let myself remain quiet. I am no saint, but that charge of Torah was a goad that would not let me hide (another way to translate the verse: "you may not hide").

Rashi, in his typical way, comments that we may not hide our eyes as though we didn't see the others' suffering.

These powerful, uncompromising, stern words call me to be who I am supposed to be. Whether tired or not, worn down or not, I can no longer hide. I must not remain indifferent.

Rabbi Bradley Shavit Artson (www.bradartson.com) holds the Abner & Roslyn Goldstine Dean's Chair at the Ziegler School of Rabbinic Studies of American Jewish University, where he is Vice President. He is the author of over twelve books, most recently *The Everyday Torah: Weekly Reflections and Inspirations* (McGraw-Hill, 2008).

A woman shall not wear a man's apparel, neither shall a man put on a woman's garment; for whosoever does these things is an abomination to the Eternal One your God.

Deuteronomy 22:5

Reclaiming Deuteronomy 22:5

As a transwoman, the verse most cited as an attack against myself and others in the transgender community is Deuteronomy 22:5. I would argue that when this is the case, it is because the verse is being misinterpreted. Most modern Christians do not understand the historical context in which the verse was written and therefore, I believe, misinterpret it and its meaning. Historically, the prohibition against women dressing as men can be easily understood as a measure to prevent women from disguising themselves as men to obtain a formal education, which was solely within the sphere of a man's world. The second half of the passage was to also prevent men from disguising themselves as women to prevent them from gaining improper access to harems and other regions of purely female domain for the purpose of sex.

I have had this text used against me, as a transwoman, by parents, family members, other relatives, and people in the general public who have tried to convince me that my being transgender was a violation of God's law, and yet they have used it due to a limited understanding of the historical nature of the Pentateuch.

From my experience, for the modern male crossdressers, the desire to dress as a woman is primarily for emotional stability and release from masculine pressures of their everyday lives. For the transgender it is the overriding need to live their lives socially as directed by their brains, a physiological condition where in fetal development, the baby develops a brain structure and identity of self contrary to the physical body. So in both of these cases the modern day understandings have no relationship to the reasoning behind the restrictions or limitations as set down in Deuteronomy 22:5, and therefore have no bearing today.

For the sake of myself and those in the trans community I have come to strongly believe that we need to educate faith leaders so that we can become communities of inclusion, acceptance and understanding, rather than communities which try to force one another into molds that don't fit based on interpretations of text that don't take into consideration contemporary understandings. Far too much damage has been done over the centuries to transgenders everywhere because of this misunderstanding, in many cases excluding them from a free and open relationship with G-D within the framework of religion.

This is the verse which has so impacted me in my life and about which I try to educate others.

Reverend Megan More received her Master of Divinity at Claremont School of Theology in May 2011 and was ordained in the UFMCC in the spring of 2012. She is also active with a transgender ministry, working to educate the greater community through online services and public speaking on transgenders and faith.

You shall not subvert the rights of the stranger or the fatherless; and you shall not take the widow's garment in pawn. But you shall remember that you were a slave in Egypt, and the Eternal One your God redeemed you from there; therefore I command you to do this thing. When you reap your harvest in your field, and you have forgotten a sheaf in the field, you shall not go back to fetch it; it shall be for the stranger, for the fatherless, and for the widow; that the Eternal One your God may bless you in all the work of your hands. When you beat your olive tree, you shall not go over the boughs again; it shall be for the stranger, for the fatherless, and for the widow. When you gather the grapes of your vineyard, you shall not glean it after yourself; it shall be for the stranger, for the fatherless, and for the widow. And you shall remember that you were a slave in the land of Egypt; therefore I command you to do this thing.

Deuteronomy 24:17–22

"Remember, You Were a Slave . . ."

This instruction to the people in the Book of Deuteronomy has come to be known as the Hospitality Code. It is repeated and referenced numerous times in the Hebrew Bible and the Christian Testament. As such it is foundational to both Jewish and Christian ethics. This teaching is about power and vulnerability, fundamental to the human condition and to our relationships with each other.

Not merely an altruistic extension of the Golden Rule, it is an obligation based on the reminder that "you were a slave in Egypt." You know what it is like to be vulnerable and to need help. So when someone else is vulnerable and you have the capacity to help, you are obligated to do so. When you are again vulnerable (and you will be), there will be someone there for you.

The Hospitality Code provides a basis for our understanding of addressing sexual and domestic violence which is the focus of my ministry. Those who are most vulnerable, particularly women and children, deserve protection and justice. This is our obligation as faith communities. This is the teaching which guides me every day.

Reverend Dr. Marie M. Fortune is a pastor in the United Church of Christ and is Founder and Senior Analyst of FaithTrust Institute (www.faithtrustinstitute.org). She is a writer and educator, practicing ethicist and theologian. Her books include *Keeping the Faith: Questions and Answers for Christian Abused Women* and *Sexual Violence: The Sin Revisited.*

Blessed shall you be in your comings and blessed shall you be in your goings.

Deuteronomy 28:6

Comings and Goings

Many years ago, under the guidance of my friend and mentor, Rabbi Edward E. Klein *z"l*, I chose these words as the final ones I would recite at the end of every service. Even today, my benediction consists of a moment of silent meditation, then a few words of prayer appropriate for the occasion, and then this verse from Deuteronomy in Hebrew and in English. To me, these words express the hope that as we are blessed by the realization of God's Presence when we come into the sanctuary so that Presence, the *Shechinah*, will remain with us throughout the week as we face the challenges of everyday.

Over the years, my congregants came to expect these words at the end of the service and often the children would mouth them with me. They also came to expect the eye-to-eye contact that accompanied the words as my gaze went from one person to the next connecting with each worshipper and cementing the relationship that made us part of one community. Now that I am retired I notice that when I am invited to offer the benediction the members of my temple family anticipate these words and respond with smiles when I get to them.

Our sages noted that the verse is written in the plural when the singular would have been sufficient. Among the many interpretations is one suggesting that the reference here is to the ultimate coming and going—birth and death—our first entrance into the world and our final exit. Rabbi Berekiah explained this to mean: "Happy are those whose time of death is like the time of their birth. Just as at the time of their birth they are free from sin, so too at the time of their death they are free from sin" (*Midrash Rabbah*).

For me, this serves as a reminder that the legacy we leave behind is one we create for ourselves. How we are characterized at birth depends upon others. How we are characterized at death depends upon us. Every moment is an opportunity to be helpful or hurtful, caring or cruel—and when we choose to live up to our highest selves, then we are worthy of the blessing that comes when we embrace the values of Torah.

Rabbi Sally J. Priesand, America's first female rabbi, was ordained in 1972 at the Cincinnati campus of Hebrew Union College–Jewish Institute of Religion. Following her retirement in 2006, she became Rabbi Emerita of Monmouth Reform Temple in Tinton Falls, New Jersey.

You stand this day, all of you, before the Eternal One your
God: your heads, your tribes, your elders, and your officers,
every man of Israel; your little ones, your women, and your
stranger that is in the midst of your camp, from the wood-
chopper to the water-drawer.

Deuteronomy 29:9–10

Belonging

From the time I first read these words as a young boy, I have
been drawn to this passage and its meaning as the ancient rabbis
understood it. As a Jewish boy who grew up in the South, they
have spoken to me in a profound way of the universal human
need all of us have to belong. Let me explain.

The verses, expressed by Moses as his life nears its end,
clearly intend to be inclusive. Moses addresses the entirety of
the Jewish people, "from the hewer of wood to the drawer of
water." Yet, a paradox emerges.

If the passage is meant to be all-encompassing, this final
phrase it seems is surely problematic. Indeed, it would have
been more logical for the phrase to have read, "from the greatest among you to the least." Instead, it seems to be non-
inclusive, specifying two groups that have seemingly low status
tasks assigned them, "from the hewer of wood to the drawer of
water."

The rabbinic writers on this passage resolve this paradox by
maintaining that the phrase, "from the hewer of wood to the
drawer of water," is in fact inclusive. They identify the "hewer
of wood" as none other than Abraham. As it says of Abraham
the first Jew in Genesis 22:3, "Then he split the wood for the
offering."

The rabbis then identify the "drawer of water" as Elijah the Prophet, who is viewed in Jewish tradition as the one who will announce the coming of the Messiah at the end of days. As it says in the passage recited at the *Havdalah* ceremony at the conclusion of the Sabbath and in which the name of the prophet Elijah is invoked with the hope that the end of history will come and that a messianic period will commence, "With joy you will draw water from the springs of salvation" (Isaiah 12:3).

In sum, the passage is fully comprehensive of the Jewish story, extending from Abraham, with whom Jewish history begins, to Elijah, who will herald the end of historical existence. The passage thus bespeaks the bonds that bind all generations of Jews as one.

These verses thus express the solidarity I so cherish that marks unity of the Jewish people, and they capture the aspirations I have as a human being to affirm my own roots and identity by belonging to a specific community, even as I recognize and celebrate the diversity that marks humankind.

Rabbi David Ellenson is President of Hebrew Union College–Jewish Institute of Religion. His new book, with Daniel Gordis, is *Pledges of Jewish Allegiance: Conversion, Law, and Policymaking in Nineteenth- and Twentieth-Century Orthodox Responsa* (Stanford University Press, 2012).

It is not in heaven, that you should say: "Who shall go up
for us to heaven, and bring it to us, and cause us to hear it,
that we may do it?"

Deuteronomy 30:12

Not in Heaven

The Torah is not in Heaven, Torah is here on Earth.

One of the best illustrations of this sentence is the Yiddish story by I. L. Peretz "If Not Higher." In this story a skeptical Jew of Lithuanian descent is determined to disprove the holiness of the Rebbe of Nemirov as part of his plan to defeat the Hasidic movement, and prove that these "holy men" are nothing but frauds. He chooses the Rebbe of Nemirov because his followers have the most outlandish belief about their Rebbe. They believe that during the Ten Days of Repentance, from Rosh Hashanah to Yom Kippur, the Rebbe ascends to heaven to plead with God on their behalf.

A skeptic follows the Rebbe before dawn and watches as the Rebbe dons peasant clothes, chops a tree into firewood, and carries the load on his back to a broken down shack. An elderly, homebound woman opens the door and the Rebbe proceeds to make a fire in the woman's wood stove. As he stacks the wood the Rebbe whispers the High Holiday prayer.

The Rebbe's act of charity and compassion convinces the skeptic to become one of the Rebbe's greatest disciples. Later, when the former skeptic is asked if his Rebbe really goes to Heaven during the Ten Days of Repentance, the skeptic replies, "If not higher!"

Sometimes we believe that by following prescription, we can achieve the greatest spiritual heights. We convince ourselves that the way to piety, spiritual growth, and amazing heights of inspiration is based in meditation, absorption in prayer and devotion. And while all these are blessed and beautiful paths, often the most spiritual path is the one that is not about us at all.

The Rebbe of Nemirov ascended to the highest spiritual heights by demonstrating the spiritual essence of the Holy Days and the essence of Torah—love thy fellow as thyself.

The Torah is lofty in vision and idealism, but also grounded here on Earth. The Torah is not in Heaven, it is here on Earth, in the messy, imperfect world that God placed us here to fix.

Yonah Bookstein, a leading voice of the next generation of American Jewry, is an internationally recognized expert in Jewish innovation, founder of the Jewlicious Festival, and executive rabbi at JConnectLA. Rabbi Yonah is a frequent contributor to JewishJournal.com, Jewlicious.com and HuffingtonPost.com. Follow him on Twitter @RabbiYonah.

*I call heaven and earth to witness against you this day, that
I have set before you life and death, the blessing and the
curse; therefore choose life, that you and your seed may
live; to love the Eternal One your God, to hear God's voice,
and to hold fast to God; for that is your life, and the length
of your days; that you may dwell in the land which the
Eternal One swore to your fathers, to Abraham, to Isaac,
and to Jacob, to give them.*

Deuteronomy 30:19–20

Finding Hope

These verses have informed my life and still do.

I was very young when I first heard this piece of scripture.
Life in our house was not always as good as it could be. There
was a lot of arguing and unrest. My home was not secure; it was
as if we lived on the edge of falling into a black hole. I had at
that time some wonderful teachers, both nuns and priests who
were always willing to listen, and they taught me stories from
the scriptures. I lapped up the stories and was a willing learner,
always wanting to hear more.

From them I learned of Abraham and Sarah, Moses, Elijah,
and of course being Christian, Jesus. The stories became woven
into my life: I counted stars with Abraham and Sarah, walked
through the desert with Moses, met the widow and her son with
Elijah, and took Mary as my friend. The scriptures' stories were
more than stories, they were a way that I connected with God
and a world beyond my home. The particular scripture that I
have chosen became woven into my being.

My teachers helped me to see that I had choices, and then
through the stories they helped me to see how to choose life,
how to find hope in the midst of darkness. This particular piece

of scripture remains in my heart like a touchstone, always there, always with me, a guide to life, love, and hope.

The Reverend Maryalice Sullivan is a woman, a wife, a mother, a grandmother, a priest, and a spiritual director. It continues to be a privilege for her to be a priest and teacher. She has been ordained for twenty years, fourteen of those as rector of Grace Episcopal Church in North Attleboro, Massachusetts. Her own spiritual life continues to deepen as she works with people in their joy and their grief and everything in between. In the last couple of years she has continued her studies to be a spiritual director which has added new dimensions to her own journey with God.

Choose Life, Even If It Doesn't Seem as Heroic

Early in my priesthood I requested from my Provincial Superior an assignment to work with and among the Native Peoples of the Pacific Northwest. This was and is a wonderful apostolic work. It was after all at the invitation of the Flathead Tribe that Jesuits first moved into that part of the country. But over five years of ministry the work proved to be too difficult for me personally. Initially, I thought I should tough it out and not "fail" in my first assignment. Of course, I was not thinking: "Does God want me to tough this out?"

It was an apostolic work I had wanted to pursue in part because it was difficult, and few Jesuits were asking to be assigned to do it. After experiencing how I was diminishing in health, however, it became clear that I was metaphorically if not actually choosing death.

As a priest and, indeed, as a person of faith, suffering comes to me along my journey of faith. This was true for Abraham,

Isaac and Jacob, for Moses and the Israelites, and for my other ancestors in faith, the Christians throughout the centuries.

However, the suffering I passed through in my first assignment was a suffering I had brought upon myself, because I was not honoring my own personal makeup, my giftedness, and my vocation as a Jesuit.

This passage from Deuteronomy, at some point, captured the initial "choice" I had made, and invited me to reconsider my apostolic work.

From then on, I have trusted the person I know myself to be, and worked to understand fully the gifts God has given me. And, as a Jesuit, I have attempted to make that known to my superiors, so that all my subsequent assignments have been, for me, life-giving. They have not been devoid of suffering, but I have had the confidence of knowing that my work, and whatever my suffering, was where God was calling me, and not where I, in my vain cleverness, thought I should be.

I have been graced by God to know that God's desire for me surely is "life, that I and my descendants may live."

Father Patrick Conroy, S.J. is a member of the Oregon Province of Jesuits and currently serves as the Chaplain to the United States House of Representatives. He was born in Everett, Washington and graduated from Claremont Men's College before joining the Jesuit Order. He was ordained in 1983 and has a law degree and masters degrees in Philosophy and Theology.

And Moses called to Joshua and he said to him before the eyes of all Israel: "Be strong and of good courage for it is you who shall come with this people into the land which the Eternal One swore to their ancestors to give to them; and cause them to inherit it."

Deuteronomy 31:7

Be Strong and of Good Courage
Chazak v' Ematz

In chapter 31 of the Book of Deuteronomy, the Hebrew phrase *chazak v'ematz* (often translated as "Be strong and of good courage") occurs in three different places—and at three critical moments in the life of the people of Israel and its leaders. First, as God's way of reassuring the Israelites that the divine presence will never leave them, no matter what challenges they will face; second, when Moses transfers the mantle of leadership to his untested warrior-successor, Joshua, in front of the assembled multitudes; and third, as a heavenly command, again to Joshua, to go forth without fear and boldly lead his people past their adversaries and into the Promised Land.

These two Hebrew words have inspired and supported me throughout most of my life and my rabbinate. When I was younger, I would say them to myself before (or after) experiencing some adrenaline-fueled adventure, like running into a grizzly or jumping out of an airplane. When I became the founding rabbi of a new synagogue in Manhattan, I reminded myself of these words as I anxiously assumed the position of spiritual leader of my congregation. In the aftermath of the terrorist attacks on 9/11, I recited this phrase to myself and others as I tried to counsel first responders at Ground Zero. And it was these two ancient, powerful words that helped to comfort me when I went through my divorce—and the unease and uncertainty that were left in its wake.

Chazak v'ematz has served as my existential mantra, a literary gift that has helped to guide me through the dark forest, and the terror, of transition.

Chazak v'ematz has not allowed me to think that I am alone.

Whenever I do book signings, these are the words that I will usually write down on the author's page before I add my signature. I write them because they—and the messages that they convey—are at the heart and soul of all of my own works: We must never give up hope; we are never alone; faith will always triumph over fear.

Niles Elliot Goldstein, the founding and emeritus rabbi of The New Shul in New York City, is the award-winning author or editor of nine books, including *Gonzo Judaism: A Bold Path for Renewing an Ancient Faith*.

"Give ear, O heavens, and I will speak;
And let the earth hear the words of my mouth.
My doctrine shall drop as the rain,
My speech shall distill as the dew;
As the small rain upon the tender grass,
And as the showers upon the herb.
For I will proclaim the name of the Eternal One;
Give Glory to our God. . . ."

Deuteronomy 32:1–3

I Am, You Are

I have an affinity and appreciation for Moses as we have shared the experience of God's presence and God's speech, even to the reception of details which would not have been known if not for the presence of the living God. It may be bold and perhaps ludicrous to put myself in the same category as Moses. Yet God has graced me with His summons, welcomed me on my arrival and blessed me with His company. In doing so He moved me clearly from the concept of God to affirmation of divine company. The most important lesson in my experience was to listen, and to prompt other followers to listen for there surely is a God who continues to speak and offer direction.

No, I am no Moses. But I *am* Dave Wasemann. And God cared enough about me along with the souls I will accompany, to give me the confidence of faith and the surety of witness, and never, never to understand my witness as a vehicle for debating, persuading, or winning. I was to leave my experience with God with the notion of returning often to the presence of the living Lord, offering my heart and my words, sorting my thoughts and cares, in order to prompt other people to awaken, be aware and alert.

If anything, I could now prepare people to take the time for stillness and solitude with the assurance they weren't casting thoughts into a black hole. I am humbled and happy to be the bridge for people to meet and greet the Lord. I have even met people unexpectedly who suddenly shared a need with me or a question, and I was able to affirm the presence of God and the essence of God's communication.

I don't really care if anyone remembers my name, but I hope they will continue to appreciate one humble servant who had a spark of the flame of life which he bore to any who wished to be in touch with the source.

Pastor Dave Wasemann was ordained in 1991 in the Evangelical Lutheran Church in America (ELCA). He currently serves the Grove Chapel Harmony Grove Lutheran Parish in Indiana County, Pennsylvania.

*And Moses went up from the plains of Moab to Mount
Nebo, to the summit of Pisgah, which is opposite Jericho.
And the Eternal One showed him all the land, even Gilead
as far as Dan.*

Deuteronomy 34:1

From the Mountaintop

Almost twenty years ago I found myself atop a hillside in
Jordan looking out across a great valley. In the distance through
the haze I could see into the Promised Land just as Moses
viewed it thousands of years earlier. No map could convey how
seamlessly the valley connects the two territories on either bank
of the Jordan River. Standing there in person, Israel seemed so
close you could reach out and touch it.

Life is filled with longing for what is beyond one's reach.
Whenever I read in Deuteronomy of Moses looking out from
the same mountain, Mount Nebo, I am filled with great sadness.
I can understand why it was the end of his time of leadership. I
can accept that death comes to us all. That does not cancel out
the sorrow. I was in my 40s, healthy, yet already I could see that
in my own lifetime many of my dreams would be left unful-
filled.

There was additional sorrow that day when I stood on that
holy mountain. The sorrow of seeing how the land on both
sides was of one piece in its natural state, and yet the nations
that occupied it were not yet at peace. Soon Jordan and Israel
would sign a peace agreement, but the valley and the political
realities still separate two peoples who should be able to reach
across the divide. I have returned twice more to that mountain,
but the haze is still there. Was it there in the days of Moses?

Will it perhaps disappear when true peace and friendship take hold between Israel and her neighbors?

In the Torah verse God shows Moses all the land. It is not possible to see all the way from Gilead to Dan, according to the scientists. Perhaps Moses had to see with his heart. And perhaps that is the way each of us has to visualize the way to peace, even when it seems impossible.

Rabbi Debra R. Hachen, ordained in 1980 from Hebrew Union College–Jewish Institute of Religion, is currently the spiritual leader of Temple Beth-El in Jersey City, New Jersey. As a child in 1965, she fell in love with the land of Israel when her family spent a summer in Jerusalem and toured the country with the historian and geographer, Zev Vilnay *z"l*.

And the Eternal One said to him: "This is the land which I swore to Abraham, to Isaac, and to Jacob, saying, 'I will give it to your seed.' I have caused you to see it with your eyes, but you shall not cross over there." So Moses the servant of the Eternal One died there in the land of Moab, according to the word of the Eternal One. And God buried him in the valley in the land of Moab opposite Beth-peor; and no one knows his burial place to this day.

Deuteronomy 34:4–6

Dreams and Responsibilities

I selected this passage because I had a profound experience preaching on this text. It all seemed so tragic when God allowed Moses to see the Promised Land, but he was not allowed to "cross over there." This was something Joshua would do. Moses led the Hebrew people out of Egypt and the promise of this land and God's provision kept his people going while in the wilderness. Moses did all this work and it seemed like as a leader he deserved to fulfill his dream of leading the people into the Promised Land.

What I realized after reflecting on this story, was that Moses did not need to fulfill his dream because he had fulfilled his responsibilities. He fulfilled the role of leading the people out of Egypt and away from slavery. He also helped to lead the people through the wilderness as they faced numerous challenges. Entering the Promised Land would be filled with new challenges, and the baton of leadership needed to be passed on to a new leader and a new generation.

In life we tend to emphasize fulfilling dreams more than fulfilling responsibilities. However, what this passage helped me to realize is that dreams may keep us going, but it is the fulfillment of our responsibilities that truly adds meaning and purpose to our lives. Moses did not die with any need for regret. Sure he may have regretted certain parts of his journey or aspects of his life, but in general he had fulfilled his responsibilities and lived fully and faithfully in relationship to God and God's people. This is inspiring to me as a clergyperson.

The Reverend Doug Bixby is an ordained minister in the Evangelical Covenant Church. He is the senior pastor of the Evangelical Covenant Church of Attleboro, Massachusetts. He is the author of two books: *The Honest to God Church: A Pathway to God's Grace* (Alban, 2007) and *Challenging the Church Monster: From Conflict to Community* (Pilgrim Press, 2002). He graduated from North Park Theological Seminary in Chicago in 1993 and has been serving in pastor ministry ever since.

Glossary of Terms

Abba Shaul – Jewish sage who lived in the beginning of the second century C.E. in the Land of Israel.

Aleinu – Hebrew prayer recited near the conclusion of each of the three daily services.

Archdiocese – District for which an archbishop is responsible.

Baal Shem Tov (Besht) (1698–1760) – Rabbi from the mystical tradition, considered to be the founder of Hasidic Judaism.

Bava Metzia – Tractate of Talmud which discusses civil matters such as property law, charging of interest, and obligations related to lost property.

Ben Azai – Jewish sage who lived in the beginning of the second century C.E. in the Land of Israel.

Brakhot – First tractate of Talmud. Primarily addresses topics related to prayers and blessings.

Cheshvan – Eighth month in the Hebrew calendar (occurs in October–November in the Gregorian calendar).

Diocese – District under the supervision of a bishop.

Eyn Yaakov – Compilation of the non-legalistic material in the Talmud with commentaries.

Gospel of John (The Gospel According to John) – An account of the public ministry of Jesus beginning with John the Baptist and ending with the death and resurrection of Jesus and his post-resurrection appearances.

Haftarah – Reading from the Book of Prophets which follows the reading from Torah on the Sabbath and Jewish holidays. There is often some thematic or other relationship between the Torah reading and the haftarah for any given day.

Haran (also Charan) – Biblical stopping place for Abraham on his way to Canaan.

HaShem – Hebrew for "The Name," a reference to God.

Hasidic (masters) – Orthodox leaders of various sects who led and influenced many followers. The Hasidic movement was born in 18th century Eastern Europe.

Havdalah – Prayer service/ceremony marking the end of the Jewish Sabbath.

Hebrews – Book of the Christian Bible focusing on Christ and his role as mediator between God and humanity.

Heschel, Abraham Joshua (1907–1972) – American rabbi and leading Jewish theologian and philosopher, also known for his commitment to social action causes and civil rights.

Hevruta – Pair of individuals engaged in Jewish text study (also refers to one's partner in the study).

Hillel – Renowned Jewish religious leader, sage, and scholar, many of whose opinions are recorded in the Talmud. Born in Babylonia in the first century B.C.E., he later migrated to the Land of Israel.

Ibn Ezra (1089–1167) – Greatly respected commentator on the Torah and other books of the Bible.

Icon – Religious image used in the devotions of Eastern Christians.

Jesuit – Member of the Society of Jesus, a Catholic male religious order which follows the teachings of the Catholic Church.

Kabbalah – Jewish mysticism and the mystical school of thought.

Kibbutz – A type of collective farm, found in Israel.

Kiddush – Hebrew, meaning "sanctification," the ritual blessing over wine or grape juice.

Kippah – Hebrew term for yarmulke, the headcovering worn by many Jews when they pray, study, or recite blessings and by some Jews at all times.

Kotzker Rebbe (1787–1859) – Hasidic rabbi and leader.

Ma'ariv – Hebrew, referring to the evening prayer service.

Machzor – Prayerbook specifically used by Jews on the High Holidays (Rosh Hashanah and Yom Kippur). There are also versions for the holidays of Sukkot, Passover, and Shavuot.

Mehilta Shirta – A section of the Hebrew commentary on the Book of Exodus.

Midrash – Collection of non-legal writings on the books of the Hebrew Bible.

Midrash Tanhuma – Name given to three different collections of commentaries on the Five Books of Moses.

Mishnah – Compilation by Rabbi Judah HaNasi of the laws of the Torah, organized by topic.

Mourner's Kaddish – Hebrew prayer which is recited by those in mourning.

Mussar – Jewish movement focusing on ethics and moral conduct that developed in 19th century Eastern Europe. Mussar writings date back to the 11th century C.E.

Nehirim – National community of LGBT Jews (and straight and non-Jewish allies) committed to creating a more inclusive and just religious world.

Oral Torah – Legal and interpretive law believed to have been transmitted orally at Mount Sinai (eventually recorded in the Mishnah, Talmud, and Midrash).

Parish – Geographic area under jurisdiction of a priest. Also refers to the people of that community and the church property as well.

Philo (20 B.C.E.–50 C.E.) – Jewish biblical philosopher born in Alexandria.

Picpus Fathers – A Catholic religious order also known as the Congregation of the Sacred Hearts of Jesus and Mary. It was founded on Christmas Eve in 1800 and consists of priests, brothers, and nuns. Picpus is the street name in Paris where they had their first home. The initials SS.CC. refer to the plural Latin form (initials) of "Sacred Hearts."

Rabbi Berekiah – Jewish sage who lived in the Land of Israel in the fourth century C.E.

Rabbi Ishmael (90–135 C.E.) – Rabbinic scholar whose views are recorded in the Mishnah.

Rabbi Nachman of Bratslav (Breslov) (1772–1810) – Founder of the Breslov Hasidic movement. His philosophy revolved around a personal, joyful connection and closeness to God.

Rabbi Yohanan – Torah scholar who lived around the time 200 C.E.

Rabbi Yochanan ben Zackai (30–90 C.E.) – Important Jewish sage and a primary contributor to the Mishnah.

Rashi – Medieval French rabbi, author of a comprehensive commentary on the Talmud and a comprehensive commentary on the Hebrew Bible.

Rebbe – Master, teacher, or mentor; a Yiddish word derived from the Hebrew word Rabbi.

Rector – Director, often of a religious seminary.

Resh Lakish – Torah scholar who lived around the time 200 C.E.

Sanhedrin – The Jewish court system in ancient Israel. It lasted until approximately 425 C.E.

Seder – The ritual Passover dinner, from the Hebrew meaning "order."

Shabbat Shirah – Hebrew, meaning "Sabbath of Song," the name given to the Sabbath on which the narrative of the crossing of the Sea of Reeds is read from the Torah.

Shechinah (also Shekhina) – A grammatically feminine Hebrew word used to refer to the presence of God in the world.

Sheen, Archbishop Fulton J. (1895–1979) – American archbishop of the Catholic Church. He was a renowned theologian and a radio and television host, including the radio show *The Catholic Hour* (1930–1950).

Sherut La'am – A program combining educational and community service opportunities in Israel for young adults (literally meaning "service for the People").

Shiva minyan – A quorum of ten or more Jewish adults (Bar/Bat Mitzvah age and older), gathered in a house of mourning to recite the daily prayers during the week following a burial.

Sh'ma (also Shema, Shma) – A central Jewish prayer, the theme of which is the belief that there is one God.

Synod – A council or an assembly of church officials or churches.

Talmud – A central text of Judaism which is a record of rabbinic discussions relating to Jewish law, ethics, philosophy, customs, and history. The Talmud was compiled between 200–500 C.E.

Tanach – Hebrew abbreviation for the three parts of the Jewish Bible—the Torah, the Prophets, and the Writings.

Torah – The first part of the Hebrew Bible (often referred to as the Pentateuch or the Five Books of Moses). Torah can refer to the handwritten scroll on which the Five Books of Moses are recorded. When written in lowercase (i.e., torah) it can be understood as a teaching.

Vestryman – A member of the leading body of one's local church.

Wesley, John – Eighteenth century Church of England cleric and Christian theologian credited (with his brother) with founding the Methodist movement.

Yahwist – One of the sources of the Five Books of Moses, according to some who believe that there were several different writers. Yahwist refers to the writer who refers to God using the four letter name for God.

Yoma – The fifth tractate of the section of the Talmud which is concerned mainly with the laws of Yom Kippur.

Z"l – Abbreviation for *zichrono livracha* or *zichrona livracha*, meaning "may his/her memory be for a blessing."

Zionist – Describes an individual or group dedicated to a love of the Land of Israel and the belief that it is the Homeland of the Jewish People.

Index of Contributors

Suggested Discussions and Follow-up Ideas

1. Choose a reflection written by a religious leader of a faith other than your own. What about it resonated with you? Were you surprised by the way you responded to it? Why?

2. Choose a theme on which a number of contributors reflected (e.g., their calling, faith, social justice). Discuss this theme as represented in the book and how it relates to and resonates with the members of your group.

3. As a group, choose one text and the clergy response to it. Share your thoughts on that reflection.

4. Was there a reflection by a clergyperson of your own faith with which you did not connect or agree? Discuss.

5. If you were to choose the passage from the Five Books of Moses which informs your life, speaks to you in a personal way, or which you consider most important, which would you choose? How has it impacted or informed your life?

6. Many of the responses from the clergy addressed the text from the perspective of their lives as religious leaders. What insights did you gain into the life and work of religious leaders?

7. Consider creating in your house of worship a book of congregant reflections similar to those in this book. Have congregants choose a text and then create a written or visual response to it. Make it an ongoing project to which congregants can add and which the congregation can display.

8. Create a mural for your congregation. Divide the mural into five sections (one for each book of the Five Books of Moses). Create an artistic symbol of the themes in each section and invite congregants to add their own reflections (written and artistic renderings) in the appropriate section.

9. Some of the contributors asked about whether they could choose a verse from one of the other sections of the Bible (e.g., Prophets, Psalms, etc.). Which verses speak to you from the other writings in Scripture?

10. If your congregation has a relationship with another faith community, consider creating a study group together to read and discuss the clergy responses in this book and to share your own personal responses to particular verses and narratives in the Five Books of Moses. This could be used to launch an interfaith book or study group.

**Continue the conversation
with the editor, contributors, and other readers at:**

SacredDialogue.blogspot.com

Acknowledgements

First, I would like to thank all those who contributed their words to this book. Some contributed with faith because they know me personally. Others were willing to sign on out of faith in someone who vouched for me and the integrity of this book. Others I approached out of the blue and were honored to be asked and agreed to contribute. I am deeply grateful to all the contributors for without their voices, this book would not exist. Their generosity of time and spirit as well as their beautifully written reflections remind me (and hopefully all of us) how many sparks of light there are in the world.

As well, I would like to offer thanks to the many friends, colleagues, and cyber connections many of whom went out of their way to reach out to their networks to introduce contributors to me and to the idea of this book. There are far too many of you to name and some of you who I may not even know helped to make the introductions, but I hope you will recognize yourself in these words and know that your efforts are greatly appreciated.

It was a discussion with Rabbi John Rosove about a previous project which sparked the idea for this book several years ago. One never knows where a conversation may lead and what creative spark it may light, so to Rabbi Rosove and the power of creative sparks and the mystery of what happens once they set the creative mind on fire, I am grateful. I am very appreciative of the Temple Aliyah leadership and community in Woodland Hills, California for their support in agreeing to a creative leave of absence during which the work on this book began. A special thank you to Rabbi Elliot Dorff, Rabbi John Rosove, Rabbi Stewart Vogel, and Monsignor Robert McNamara. In the infancy of this project each gave of his time to meet with me in person, and in addition to signing on to contribute when this book was in its genesis, each referred me to colleagues and community members. I am deeply indebted.

I want to express my gratitude to Rabbi Gary Oren and Jeff DeVore for reading over the Glossary of Terms and giving me their input.

Finally, I am so very appreciative of Sapphira Fein and Seth Rosenzweig of Blackbird Books (and to Joel Abramovitz for introducing us). Seth and Sapphira have, from the beginning, expressed an enthusiasm for this project, and every conversation and interaction has been one of mutual respect and collaboration. I am very appreciative of our professional relationship and of our budding friendship.

Thank you.

About the Editor

Jeff Bernhardt is a writer, educator, and licensed clinical social worker currently residing in Los Angeles. He earned a B.A. in Sociology and Education at Brandeis University, an MSW at USC, and an M.A. in Jewish Communal Service at Hebrew Union College. His writing has appeared in the *Journal of Jewish Communal Service*, the *Los Angeles Times*, and the *Jewish Journal* (Los Angeles), as well as Jewish newspapers throughout the United States. His work has also appeared in the books *Mentsh* (Alyson Books, 2004) and *Rosh Hashanah Readings* (Jewish Lights, 2006). He has written the dramatic readings *Who Shall Live . . . ?*, *Standing at Sinai*, and *Those Who Walked Beside Us*, which have been performed in synagogues and other Jewish communal settings throughout North America (www.jewishdramas.com). His play *Mixed Blessings* premiered in Los Angeles in 2010. He can be contacted at jmbedsw@aol.com.

To see our other great titles,
visit us at:

BLACKBIRD BOOKS
www.bbirdbooks.com

CPSIA information can be obtained at www.ICGtesting.com
Printed in the USA
LVOW052347140812

294312LV00009B/143/P